EMOTIONAL INTELLIGENCE

Everything You Need to Know to Develop Mindfulness

(A Comprehensive Guide to Improving Your Social Skills and Emotional Agility)

Irving Johnson

Published by John Kembrey

Irving Johnson

All Rights Reserved

Emotional Intelligence: Everything You Need to Know to Develop Mindfulness (A Comprehensive Guide to Improving Your Social Skills and Emotional Agility)

ISBN 978-1-77485-314-6

All rights reserved. No part of this guide may be reproduced in any form without permission in writing from the publisher except in the case of brief quotations embodied in critical articles or reviews.

Legal & Disclaimer

The information contained in this book is not designed to replace or take the place of any form of medicine or professional medical advice. The information in this book has been provided for educational and entertainment purposes only.

The information contained in this book has been compiled from sources deemed reliable, and it is accurate to the best of the Author's knowledge; however, the Author cannot guarantee its accuracy and validity and cannot be held liable for any errors or omissions. Changes are periodically made to this book. You must consult your doctor or get professional medical advice before using any of the suggested remedies, techniques, or information in this book.

Upon using the information contained in this book, you agree to hold harmless the Author from and against any damages, costs, and expenses, including any legal fees potentially resulting from the application of any of the information provided by this guide. This disclaimer applies to any damages or injury caused by the use and application, whether directly or indirectly, of any advice or information presented, whether for breach of contract, tort, negligence, personal injury, criminal intent, or under any other cause of action.

You agree to accept all risks of using the information presented inside this book. You need to consult a professional medical practitioner in order to ensure you are both able and healthy enough to participate in this program.

Table of Contents

INTRODUCTION 1

CHAPTER 1: BEING AWARE OF THYSELF 6

CHAPTER 2: HABITS OF EMPATHY 11

CHAPTER 3: UNDERSTANDING PEOPLE AROUND YOU 16

CHAPTER 4: EMOTIONAL INTELLIGENCE IN CHILDREN 30

CHAPTER 5: WHAT TO ENHANCE YOUR EMOTIONAL INTELLIGENCE 42

CHAPTER 6: EFFECTIVE EXERCISES TO IMPROVE YOUR POSITIVITY 48

CHAPTER 7: HOW EMOTIONAL INTELLIGENCE ENHANCES YOUR SELF-CONFIDENCE 58

CHAPTER 8: HOW WHAT YOU CAN DO TO HELP MAKE A DIFFERENCE 63

CHAPTER 9: REACTING WILL LEAD TO THE SAME RESULTS. PAUSING WILL LET YOU PICK YOUR RESPONSE 80

CHAPTER 10: RELEVANCE OF SELF-AWARENESS 90

CHAPTER 11: THE WAY TO BE EMOTIONALLY INTELLIGENT 94

CHAPTER 12: THE WAY OF INTIMACY 106

CHAPTER 13: DEVELOP PEOPLE SKILLS 111

CHAPTER 14: PROUD TO BE AUTHENTIC 120

CHAPTER 15: ESTABLISH ACCOUNTABILITY 124

CHAPTER 16: BUILDING EMOTIONALLY EFFECTIVE RELATIONSHIPS 131

CHAPTER 17: UNDERSTANDING OTHERS 153

CHAPTER 18: EMPATHY INTELLIGENCE AND RELATIONSHIPS 160

CHAPTER 19: WHAT THINGS MENTALLY STRONG PEOPLE DO NOT DO 167

CONCLUSION 183

Introduction

We tend to see ourselves as practical, rational creatures. We base our daily activities and decisions on the assumption that our ability to rationalize can lead us to the most beneficial results. We examine our past from a present view and think about what led us choose that drunken photo from a night out and then post it on social networks.

The majority of us arrive at conclusions that may not have thought clearly the day before, but since we are capable of making a conscious, well-informed decision not to make the same mistake this time. We live our lives in accordance with this belief of planning our days so that we can get things completed; acting on the job in a manner that makes your boss see the value of our work while trying to avoid having the unpleasant conversation with our partner.

We also employ our thinking skills to make plans for our future. When we start school when we were children, go through high school, and continue into college. Higher education can increase the likelihood of securing an excellent job that can allow us to support us and our families, and perhaps even purchase an expensive automobile. The belief that our capacity to make logical, sensible decisions is the only thing you need to live an enjoyable and successful life is a misconception that most of us.

Though the intellect, or reason is an essential part of our human nature but it is crucial to think about the vital role that emotion plays in our daily lives. The emotions we experience influence our daily choices and actions, even those that are rational.

Let's say, for instance, you're on your way to work. You're in a hurry due to the fact that you've slept through your alarm clock. Then, someone stops you on the road. The majority of us will be angry, frustrated or even mad, and in good faith. Who is that person thinking that he is? However, this emotional outburst could have a direct impact on our reaction to a semi-truck stopping abruptly before us. When you are enraged, you may not be able to hit the breaks on time, and an accident could be inevitable.

What would happen If we could manage our emotions? Perhaps the driver who sped off from you is heading to the hospital to visit his father who is dying in the final hours in his existence. However, even if that's not the case, being empathetic in these kinds of situations instead of immediately rushing into anger offers you the chance to prevent the incident.

We've all been through situations where our emotions led us to make poor choices or make mistakes. This is due to the state of our emotions can influence every aspect of our lives from interviews for jobs to romantic evenings with your loved one.

The rationality of everything you have made could be wasted if you didn't recognize and comprehend your state of mind. It's true that people are emotional, regardless of regardless of whether we acknowledge that or not. We have the ability to be able to discern the emotions of other people. Some people are better than others, while others haven't yet realized their full potential.

Understanding how to access these states of mind which we aren't paying focus on can help us determine the way we react to certain circumstances. In this way it is possible to avoid daily stress could be reduced drastically. The ability to control your emotions and understand the emotions of others may give us the chance to find true happiness , free of all the stress and burdens from the past.

Being more aware of ourselves regarding others can lead to better relationships and more success in our work. Although rational intelligence plays an important part in our lives, it's equally important (if not more so) to be able to think in the realm of emotional intelligence.

Chapter 1: Being aware of Thyself

If we are confronted with the question "Who do you think that is?" we usually take an instant to think about the answer. Most of the time we can't answer directly since we don't know much about our own identity.

Being self-aware is simply knowing your personal character and emotions. Self-awareness means having a clear view of your strengths as well as weaknesses, thoughts, and ideas. Self-awareness helps you know those you meet as well as interact with. You can go as far as to say that self-awareness is the first step in becoming a master of your own life.

What's this to do with emotional intelligence? The development of self-awareness is among the first steps towards developing the emotional intelligence. Self-awareness cannot be developed without looking at your past and present self.

Building Self-Awareness

These are steps to improving your self-awareness.

Self-reflection. Develop a habit of daily self-reflection. Know your identity and the things you are doing. Each night, before going to bed, give yourself at least 10 minutes to consider everything you've gone through and accomplished during the course of your day. This helps you concentrate only on the essential parts of your day and assist you in establishing your priority issues. You can reflect on your life in numerous ways. You can speak to a person write a diary and take long walks through nature or simply gaze outside at serene scenery.

Meditate. Meditation is one of the most effective methods to develop self-awareness. It can take you to a higher place than the earth. It allows you to concentrate on your inner self. Meditation creates a feeling of calm and peace you've never experienced before. And within the trance of peace is where you will discover the truth about your life and the real you. Meditation helps you focus on the most important things and create a sense of being healthy and well.

Request feedback from other people. As we said earlier, we all have our own perspectives and ideas that make us different from each other. It is important to talk with others to learn the things they see in us, and also recognize the things we don't see within our own lives. These are commonly referred to as blind spots. It is possible to access those blind spots through asking those around us for their valuable opinions about us, and their opinions about ourselves as a person, as a human being, an individual in the family as well as a friend. While it can be difficult to accept some criticisms however, we should be able to put our emotions aside and concentrate on what others say about us in order to become completely self-aware.

Self-Awareness as an Ability

Self-awareness is a powerful leadership ability. It is the foundation of one's personal growth and accomplishment. It is, in fact, the primary aspect of our subject Emotional intelligence. Self-awareness can transform one's life. It helps one see the world in a more logical manner. When you are aware of yourself it's difficult for your feelings to overtake your life. Although it might be, we are actually the prisoner of our thoughts. Fear of emotional triggers and traps are all in the mind. After that's conquered the person will be free from anything that keeps them behind. Confidence and control of emotions is achievable once you begin believing in yourself.

To ensure that we're not enslaved by our thoughts and to ensure our freedom to be free, we need to understand our own behavior and how we respond to events and individuals. Self-awareness is the primary domain of emotional intelligence. it is essential to begin by gaining insight into our self-awareness. This is the way to lead our success.

Chapter 2: Habits Of Empathy

Another important aspect of emotion intelligence lies in empathy. The way you feel isn't solely about what's in you , but also about how other people who are around you feel. By becoming aware you are more aware of other people's thoughts, and are more mindful when making an acquaintance.

These are the behaviors that make people who are emotionally intelligent more trustworthy and likable.

9. They show sensitivity to how others feel.

They take into account the opinions of other people when they make a choice or take an action. They stop when they believe that someone might be hurt in a way that is not necessary, particularly when it's for their own pleasure or satisfaction. They consider which is more important over time: what they feel or how others might think, and also the things they would like to do or what others need. They stay clear of doing things they do not wish others to cause harm to them.

Application: Consider the personality of those whom you will impact by your actions. Are they sensitive? What are their reactions to criticism, jokes, and innuendoes? What are the limits of their acceptance of what is right and proper? Be aware of the limits of their acceptance and apply it to your own interactions with them. Do not offend others just for the sake of your own pleasure.

10. They help other people avoid the danger of emotional turmoil.

People who are emotionally intelligent have an emotions of altruism. They don't want to place other people in a uncomfortable circumstance, like an embarrassing and uncomfortable situation. If they observe someone getting caught in a situation and they decide to do something to protect the person from the emotional stress.

Application The goal is to be the hero of an individual whenever you find yourself in a stressful situation. Alter the subject, speak to defend him, or do whatever to make the situation more pleasant and divert attention from the person. The moment you save his face, it can make him feel he owes you a favor.

11. They acknowledge the feelings of others by acknowledging their responsibility.

Their compassion for others allows them to understand the feeling of be a victim of a negative reaction They take the responsibility for any time they caused someone else to be in a predicament. They're not afraid to admit to their mistakes since they feel confident and accepted. They don't let their bad emotions linger in their mind and can move on after admitting that they were accountable.

Application Resolve to apologize whenever you are required to however, don't offer excuses that don't alter the harm that has already been caused. Don't wait for someone else to come to your attention prior to acknowledging and apologize, as this marks you as a snob.

12. They are aware of that emotional demands of others.

They offer a listening ear whenever someone needs someone to listen. They offer their opinion when someone is in need of opinions or advice. They remain cool when they see someone getting hot, to ease the impending chaos. They offer a shoulder to people need someone to cry on. They are the person someone requires to meet their emotional desires. They're not selfish They strive to demonstrate whenever they can that they're an ally regardless of what the circumstance is, offering support but not judgement when necessary.

Application: Consider what type of support people around you require. If you notice someone is struggling with emotions due to feelings of anger, sadness and unease it is your responsibility to be a calming person and allow him to let his emotions flow. The same applies when he is too enthusiastic to speak about things with you. Encourage someone to express his opinions however, be aware of the only thing he requires is silence and your presence , or your advice and opinion.

Help others to feel better, so you can get reciprocation later on. Some moments are not just solely about you. Certain moments are for others, and you are in the background , helping others.

Chapter 3: Understanding People Around You

Understanding how to identify and recognize emotions and emotions among the people around you is as crucial to achieving happiness and success as understanding and knowing your own. However, we are social creatures, and everything we do (or not do) impacts our social interactions. Our abilities to comprehend the intentions of others, as well as their emotions can help us have more secure, stable relationships.

Imagine a friend that came to talk with you because she was unhappy about a split with her lover. If you can feel what she is feeling and understand her feelings, you can provide her with more advice, or, perhaps you should take her advice. You are aware of the emotions it can trigger within a person. You may have been through it. You know precisely what someone is in need of in this circumstance to feel better and be able to get over the trauma. You are able to take on her shoes.

Your friend will appreciate this more than you'd expect. This will help strengthen your friendship and give you an enjoyable social setting which is beneficial to the two of you.

As an alternative, imagine your coworker is trying to get responsibility for the work you did. You could certainly be embarrassed by him doing this. But knowing how it could feel in his shoes, you can instead discuss this in private. Your colleague will appreciate it perhaps even apologize and you'll be happier for it. This is why the ability of empathy allowed you to enhance your personal and professional relationships that helped you live a more happiness and success generally.

Empathy

Empathy is being able to understand another's emotions and thoughts from their point of view. It is a place where you put you in someone else's shoes, feel the emotions they're experiencing and experience what they are experiencing.

Empathy helps us communicate with each other in meaningful and beneficial ways. Also the more compassionate your personality is, the more the chance you have to assist someone else by focusing on what you think is the best option from their point of view.

Research suggests that those who exhibit a high degree of empathy are more generous and attentive to the well-being of others. They also enjoy happier relationships and have more of a sense of wellbeing. This is because empathy will improve your leadership abilities and create the foundation for effective communication. It will help you develop solid and lasting professional and personal relationships.

Before diving into the subject of understanding the others who are around you, check the extent to which you're empathetic. Try answering the following questions as accurately as you can. Be aware that there isn't a either or neither of these answers.

1.) If I am you are having a chat with an acquaintance and someone asks to be part of the conversation, I can quickly discern what the other person's motives are.

We are completely in agreement (4)

Agree (3)

Do not agree (2)

Very strongly disagree (1)

2.) A friend of mine is sick, but no one to care for him until he is better. I will do all I can to assist.

Absolutely agree (4)

Agree (3)

Do not agree (2)

Very strongly disagree (1)

3)A acquaintance is waiting for me in the bar. I'm already late however, I don't really care very much. She's got time.

Absolutely agree (1)

Agree (2)

Do not agree (3)

I strongly disagree with (4)

4.) If I am part of conversations I tend to keep my attention on my personal thoughts and stories. The other people are not all that interesting.

We are 100% in agreement (1)

Agree (2)

Unanimous (3)

We strongly disagree (4)

5) I like being the focal point at any gathering.

We are 100% in agreement (1)

Agree (3)

Undecided (4)

Very strongly disagree (2)

6) I am confused by social situations.

Absolutely agree (1)

Agree (2)

Do not agree (3)

We strongly disagree (4)

7) I am able to tell when someone is lying.

We are completely in agreement (4)

Agree (3)

Unanimous (2)

Very strongly disagree (1)

8.) While watching a film I don't usually allow myself to become emotionally overwhelmed.

We are 100% in agreement (1)

Agree (2)

Unanimous (3)

I strongly disagree with (4)

9) The people I talk to often let me know when I've taken it too far when joking with somebody.

We are 100% in agreement (1)

Agree (2)

Do not agree (3)

I strongly disagree with (4)

10) I am able to detect if someone isn't liking me.

Absolutely agree (4)

Agree (3)

Do not agree (2)

Very strongly disagree (1)

Now, you can add up your scores from the test and determine what category you fall into:

30-40 points: Understanding people is what you do best.

Being able to understand others is your greatest factor. It is sometimes apparent that you know them better than they do. You are aware of what they are experiencing and why they're experiencing it. You'll have no issues in using this knowledge to create your social media networks the basis of satisfaction and success.

20-29 Points: Room to improvement

You know how people function and you are aware that people feel also. But, you're not the most adept in determining the nature of those feelings as well as what it means to them. You'd rather focus on your own needs, rather than think about other people. There is possibility of improvement. The following chapters in this book will help you understand the reasons why understanding others is more important than being able to live with them.

10-19 Points: An opportunity to take a fresh strategy

Social situations can confuse your. While you are aware of certain social norms and the importance of helping others, you prefer to be your own rules. You'll need to improve your social awareness because it will greatly increase your chances of developing satisfying and lasting relationships that bring happiness and prosperity in your professional and personal life.

Understanding the basic emotions of others

In this book, earlier in the year, you were introduced to the six fundamental emotions can all of us sense and feel. Although being connected to them in your yourself is essential for having an elevated level of emotional intelligence, it's equally important to be able to spot them in others who are around you. This can significantly increase your chances of having a positive attitude towards relationships generally.

Imagine you are at an office gathering. The conversation is lively while sipping some wine and having a blast. You glance at the space and notice your colleague in what appears to be a active discussion with her boss. She's gesticulating frequently using her hands, talking loudly, and touching her with her partner frequently.

Your boss doesn't seem to be responding in a positive manner. The eyebrows are lower and dragged to one side, his lower lip is tight and his jaw's lower part juts out. Being as intelligent like that you truly are, walk up to them and engage in conversation. You shift the focus to yourself , allowing your coworker to relax a bit and give your boss the chance to walk away from the conversation.

He was clearly annoyed with the way your colleague was acting. You left a positive impression on him when you noticed that later in the evening the man wants to discuss an issue in his business which you could assist him with. Regarding your colleague; you decide to take her for a ride because she may have had a couple too many. The next day, she calls you to express her gratitude for not letting her be a sham at the event. In this case, your emotional intelligence helped you assist two people out of a stressful situation and increase your chances of future career opportunities.

Being able to recognize and interpret emotional expressions and feelings can give you a solid ability to react quickly to social situations. This skill will greatly increase the chances of having good relationships with others, which can help you to feel happier, more appreciated, and more successful in everything you undertake.

With that in mind we'll take a closer review of all six of these emotions that we talked about earlier. In this article, you'll be able to learn to spot the physical indicators of each emotion.

Surprise

The expression of surprise often expressed by raising and arched eyebrows. The skin underneath the eyebrow is stretched , and wrinkles are seen over the face. Eyelids are open, and the white area of the eye appears between the eyebrows. The jaw is usually open and the teeth split, but there isn't any tension or stretch of the mouth.

Fear

If people are afraid, they typically raise their eyebrows in a straight line. They appear as wrinkles in the middle of the forehead, in between the eyebrows. The upper eyelids are lifted while the lower ones are tight and drawn upwards. The mouth is generally wide and the lips can be slightly stretched and pulled back.

Disgust

The signs of displeasure can be seen by focusing your eyes and lips. The upper eyelids and lower lip are elevated. The cheeks can also be raised, and the nose can appear wrinkled. If you are more skilled in this way, you'll be able to see lines appearing in the skin that are below that lower part of the eyelid. The general idea behind this look is similar to the one you would make when you smell something unpleasant.

Anger

If someone feels angry, they will lower their eyebrows, and then draw their eyebrows together. The lower lip gets tense and the eyes swell. The lips could be pressed tightly together, and the corner of each facing downwards. The nostrils could be swollen in the event that the lower jaw extends out.

Happiness

Smiles are the most important indicator of happiness. The lips' corners are pulled back and upwards and the mouth can be divided. The wrinkles usually extend between the nostrils and the lips' outer edges, while cheeks are elevated. The lower eyelid could appear wrinkled or tension-filled, and you may also be able to see crow's-feet near the eyes.

Sadness

If a person feels sad, lower corners of their eyebrows are often drawn upwards and down. The skin beneath that area is tripled, with the inner corner drawn upwards. The lips' corners are drawn in and the jaw rises and the lip is pouting. Since these traits are hard to duplicate the emotion, this expression is among the most difficult to replicate.

Learning to discern facial expressions can help you build lasting and satisfying relationships. But, being able to discern emotions of others doesn't necessarily guarantee positive interpersonal relationships. You must apply your emotional intelligence into practice to benefit from it. It is important to know how the relationships you have with those close to you can contribute to your happiness and bring you to a happy and happy life.

Chapter 4: Emotional Intelligence In Children

Of course, it is natural that we're more more interested in the intelligent quotient more than the emotional quotient since we believe that an extremely intelligent quotient is everything a child requires at the beginning of his life. They are incorporated into the education system (School) and it is thought that with a high IQ the child will effortlessly excel in his studies and in the long term, in the development of his entire life.

Being a person with a high IQ is beneficial; it helps make learning more efficient and effective. However, having EQ can be the difference in the child's education and career. What's the importance of high-school grades if children aren't aware about the world? What exactly is academic excellence when a child doesn't have a clear understanding of his environment and how can they be able to get into the groove of it?

Parents will often claim that the proper care of their child is mostly focused on ensuring that he succeeds in school, but the need to develop emotional intelligence is just as (if not the most important) vital. It provides the child with the required tools to cope with any challenge that happens to him including at school, where he can learn everything.

The emotions are present each day, and it is essential to research and learn about our emotions, as well as the world's (others'). We can then learn more effectively, better understand communicate more effectively and live more effectively. As children, they are expected to understand comparatively less than grownups or adults. They are still growing into the world. So, they're bound to have a lot of questions that pop up in their heads. If your child falls into this category, then you'll need be prepared for a lot of "Dad What's the reason?" Mom, how?" The inquisitiveness is typical.

When you build emotional intelligence in children, they're equipped to communicate effectively to build effective and lasting relationships, and navigate through the tense and challenging scenarios that life will be in, and eventually to become leaders in whatever situation they find themselves in. Researchers from Stanford University found that children who had the ability to manage their impulses and regulate their behavior from a young age generally have better results in later life than those who had little self-regulation.

A greater proportion of schools concentrate more on the intelligence quotient rather than the emotional quotient. Therefore, there is the need for parents to be aware of this vital tool. Parents are the best in a position to guide their child to develop their emotional intelligence, but howcan they do that?

Methods to Enhance Emotional Intelligence of Children

Body signals are a sign of emotion and require an appropriate response. Inform your children that they shouldn't act when they are in the influence of extreme emotion. Instead they should be able to tolerate and control their emotions without having to react to them in a rash manner until they can find an appropriate way to deal with the problem. As your child ages is likely to encounter obstacles that could test his abilities. There's a chance that there will be some difficult instances that could throw children off the balance. Thus, the development of emotional intelligence is a continuous process through the childhood and adolescent years. Integrate building your sensitive skills into your daily routine. Make use of your child's mistakes to provide opportunities to grow and learn. With your ongoing help and guidance, your child will build the mental and emotional strength to achieve success in the world.

Encourage your child to recognize their own feelings

The initial step in developing Emotional Intelligence in children is to assist them understand and recognize their emotions. This ability is essential for their ability to communicate their emotions and explain the state of their emotions in a way that is appropriate.

Learn to teach your child to identify and assign labels to his feelings. If, for instance, you suspect that a child may be unhappy after an unpleasant experience You can tell him, "oh boy, it appears you're extremely angry right now. Does that sound right?". Continue using everyday occasions to increase his emotional vocabulary until he comprehends the entire process. Make sure that you can understand positive and negative emotions.

Once a child has done this right, he begin to take responsibility and identifying emotions that are embarrassing or unacceptable.

Also, if your child is upset be sure to let him know in the context of how his feelings are impacting him in relation to other people. Explain why it caused him to feel this way and then describe the emotion. If you can help your child name his emotions and think about the reasons behind them, you're bolstering the child's resistance to emotional disturbances.

Research suggests that helping children identify their emotions may have an effect of calming the nervous system. It helps them recuperate more quickly from stressful events. Additionally, they'll be able to control their emotions and manage their reactions to events. for instance an infant can speak his frustration or anger and come up with ways to calm the emotions instead of becoming agitated and acting in an unnatural manner.

Empathy as a tool to guide us

Empathy can assist you in managing the behavior of your child in a positive manner.

Empathy allows you to understand your child's emotions and comprehend his emotions. If your child displays any emotion that is disruptive, look at things from the perspective of his child and comprehend the emotions he might be experiencing right now. You can confirm the emotions by asking him to explain why you feel that way. Show compassion even if that you don't know why he's acting in this manner. Discuss things or events which might be troubling the child's mind. Sometimes, you can find clues to a child's issues with his emotions by listening to what transpired during recent events. For example, if a child is returning from school, inquire "how did the school go today? In order to explain the school environment it is possible to include the incident that caused the irritation. When a child realizes that you're completely attentive and willing to hear the emotions that he's trying to express. He'll release the emotions, and be relaxed and work with you.

If the child is able to sense the concern and understanding of your manner of dealing, he'll speak up and offer additional information that will help you gain a better comprehension of the issue. Being understood can bring a sense of calm. Additionally, you're helping him develop a strong empathy skills by the way you relate to him.

Show the appropriate ways to express Feelings

Studies have shown that parents with a high level of emotional intelligence tend to have children who are emotionally intelligent. We must teach our children about how they can express emotions in a manner that is appropriate for them. The best method to impart these abilities is to demonstrate these abilities yourself. How you handle your emotional reactions can be a significant factor to make you a more loving, nurturing, and influential and a loving parent. The messages you convey to your child via your words and your emotions will remain in their mind. Make use of emotive expressions during your conversations with your children and make sure you are able to talk about them. If you work on your skills and some of the key emotional abilities that are applicable to parenting, such as control of impulses and empathy, you'll be a great role model that your child can follow. Determine the vital emotional skills that you must master to increase your emotional competence as parent. If you have good emotional skills are in place, you'll be able manage your own emotions as well as those from your children in a more effective way to get the best from your child. Being able to control your impulse-driven behavior could make a huge difference in helping you become a steady compassionate, loving, and efficient parent.

It is normal to feel emotional sometimes however, you shouldn't be irresponsible in your behavior. Finding yourself frustrated, hurt anger, anxious, or depressed are all part of parenting however they shouldn't be a reason to avoid the conversation. If you demonstrate a positive way of dealing with your emotions Your children are likely to take note of it.

Be a role model. Young children tend to pay at the activities happening around them, particularly how their parents behave. They want to imitate their parents. If you are engaged in a heated discussion with a friend and, in the process you lose your cool. You shouldn't be too shocked when your child behaves the same way as his schoolmate. They may even use the exact words you used to a neighbor. It is crucial to recognize that your child is looking at you as a role model, that he would like to be at least before he is old enough and decides to take a different path. To develop emotional intelligence in children, you must work to improve your own emotional quotient while you are parents.

Enhancing problem-solving skills

When a child's emotions are identified and dealt with, it's now time to think about the solution in the first place. This is an important element in developing emotional intelligence. After having thought about the best way to express their feelings they should also be able to recognize how to compromise in order to find positive solutions to issues. Parents should play the role of a coach by offering guidance as needed to finding the solution. Do not act as an expert in solving problems, but instead concentrate on developing the child's capacity to solve issues efficiently and in peace by himself.

Sometimes, children can solve this problem independently however, they may need your assistance to think of ideas. There are often many options to resolve problems. You could provide all possible solutions, but let him figure it out on his own.

If it seems that the child doesn't have the social skills needed to be a good friend to others in the larger group. It is possible to improve his social abilities by assisting him develop positive relationships with other people. This can be accomplished through arranging a game with just three or four children so that the child can practice how to relate with others.

Chapter 5: What to Enhance Your Emotional Intelligence

The information that enters your brain must first go through your senses. When this information is emotionally charged or extremely stressful the natural instincts of your brain are in charge and your capacity to make decisions is limited. In order to make the right decisions when you face situations like these it is essential to know how to control your emotions with care.

The emotional state is also closely linked to memory. If you are able to remain connected to the emotional and rational parts that is your brain you'll be able expand your options in responding to events. Additionally, integrating emotional memory into your decision-making process can help keep you from making the same mistakes.

The most important skills of emotional intelligence

If you are looking to increase your emotional intelligence and ability to make informed decisions that are based on emotion, you must know your emotions in full and learn how to handle your emotions in any circumstance. To accomplish this, you have to learn crucial skills for managing and regulating the stress level. This can be achieved by anyone who's determined to implement the skills they've acquired into their daily lives.

To alter your behavior for the long-term so that you can withstand pressure, you'll have to master the art of overcoming anxiety by maintaining emotional alertness and calm.

Rapid Stress Reduction

Stress is element of our daily life however, when it is in a tidal wave it could end up inducing a tense mind and the body. Stress may also block your ability to communicate clearly and can ultimately hinder the ability to comprehend an event in a clear and precise manner.

To remain in a state of balance, focus and at ease You must learn various methods to relax regardless of the degree of stress you're experiencing in your current life. Stress-busting is among the strategies you can utilize to manage effectively when confronted by an event that is stressful. The steps below can assist you build solid techniques for tackling stress.

Be aware of your physical response

If you're looking to learn to manage your emotions and decrease the effects of stress in your daily life you should understand how your body reacts to stressful situations. Take note of the way your body feels when you're stressed since this will allow you learn to manage the tension that occurs when stress happens. There are many different responses to stress. Some people might get angered or angry when confronted by a stressful circumstance while others may become more anxious and depressed. If you're one of those who is prone to becoming angry it is likely that you will react positively to events that relieve stress because they help to calm your mind. But, if you are prone to feel depressed when confronted by stress, engaging in things that will stimulate you can be the most effective option for you.

Study the Strategies for Stress-Busting that will benefit you.

One of the best methods to decrease stress levels quickly is to be active with your senses. Every person has their own unique way of responding to these sensory stimuli, and the trick is finding things that soothe you or excite you. If, for instance, you're a visual person then you should fill your home with images that inspire you to help fight off stress. However it is a good idea to respond to music, you could discover a favourite track of music that will aid in relaxing.

Emotional Awareness

The ability to be in touch with your emotions is an important aspect of knowing your own feelings. The ability to recognize your emotions also allows you remain relaxed and calm, even when you are in stressful situations. Many people are disengaged from their emotions as a result of their childhood experiences which taught people to shut their emotions out in stress-inducing situations.

Although we are able to deflect, alter or even numb our emotions but we aren't able to remove these feelings. No matter if we are aware of our feelings whether or not they remain. If you're not aware of your emotions of your emotions, your capacity to comprehend your needs is impeded which puts you at a greater likelihood of becoming overwhelmed in stressful situations. In order to develop emotional intelligence, you must to be in touch to your feelings and learn to accept them.

It is possible to develop your awareness of emotions at any point. Similar to any other development process, gaining emotional awareness must be gradual, beginning with stress management and eventually, finding ways to reconnect to your higher emotions. This can allow you to alter your perception of emotions and the way you react to them.

Chapter 6: Effective Exercises to Improve Your Positivity

After we've identified the tendency of our brain to be negative, it is time to begin several steps to change our thinking. We must first accept that we need to alter our thinking patterns and are capable of doing so. We've already observed positive thoughts are beneficial to our health. Science has proven this across a range of areas, from longevity to health, however, we didn't really require science to prove it. I think that a lot of us know that our negative thinking isn't making us perform in the best way possible. We've also seen through our lives how attractive it is to be with positive people rather than those who are constantly negative.

Believe that you can change things

Being able to change your thinking can be a major issue for those who are negative to over come. They may be aware that it is possible to do so but somehow , they have trained them into believing that change can be beyond their abilities which is a benefit that others possess but were not provided with. If you're one of those individuals, I would advise you to not quit. Instead, concentrate in the reality that you are determined to change your attitude and try some of the following exercises every day for a minimum of one month. I am sure that when you follow this plan, you will start to see improvements.

Start right at the BEGINNING

Begin your day with a positive attitude. Before you even get up, while you lie in a state that is only semi-awakeness, you should find three things you can be thankful for. It could be any of three things, and even if they seem like self-indulgent, do not let that put you off. Pay attention to each of those three items. You can play the three things around in your mind until you get a complete understanding of these three items. Try not to repeat the same three things each day or the exercise is likely to lose its meaning and turn into routine. Depending on the degree of hold negative thoughts have over you, it might initially be difficult but over the course of a week, the practice will be more effortless as your mind will begin to look at the little things you can be grateful for over every day.

Always be aware NEGATIVITY

When you wake up and start your daily routine, begin to train your mind to look for negative thoughts. If you see one, replace it with a idea positive. Numerous negative thoughts come back. The similar thought will appear in your mind throughout the your day. This can be viewed from a positive viewpoint because each time a negative thoughts begin, you will counter it with a different positive one so that you are sure you've grasped the issue and looked at all the positive aspects against it.

DO NOT CATASTROPHIZE

Instead of worrying about the worst-case scenario for any possible situation, flip your thinking upside down and consider the best possible outcome and how you'd handle this.

POLARIZING AND FILTERING

Two common characteristics used by negative people that should be avoided. Filtering involves consciously overstating the negative and undermining the positive, while polarizing is believing that things are either entirely positive or completely negative with nothing else in between. We all do some of both at times but as we improve in positive thinking and we have become aware of the weaknesses that cause the thought patterns that cause these feelings by applying the strategies we are currently trying to master.

Make sure to use your breathing

If you ever are feeling stressed, take a look at the negative thoughts that likely is the reason. Refrain from that thought and concentrate on breathing slowly and deeply while you are doing this. In stressful situations, our breathing gets quick and shallow in preparation in preparation for our fight or flight reaction that is inherited from the environment. The slow, deliberate, and controlled breathing eases this, and also sends increased oxygen levels to brain, allowing the more rational thinking process to occur.

FILL YOUR MIND

Keep your mind occupied with self-confidence and confidence. Be the person you would like to be, and eliminate any thoughts that come up telling that you aren't the person you want to be. Create mental affirmations like "I am a successful sell." Or "I am a caring and competent parent." These statements that are like this might seem insignificant, however they are filling your the mind with positive thoughts and filling up space that could otherwise be full of negative thought. A lot of people find it beneficial to note positive affirmations throughout their day. Writing is a physical act that we can perform almost without thinking can help keep in mind a positive idea which we would have considered as if it was just a running through our thoughts.

DATE THE Positive

Be sure to not just have positive thoughts, but also to use positive language in conversations. You must begin to display positive and confident personality. Just thinking positively isn't enough. If you wish to reap the maximum benefits of having a positive outlook, you have to be perceived by others as positive in the way you go about your daily life. This has two advantages. It makes you concentrate on the positive whenever you speak to yourself, and it can create an environment of positive vibes amongst the people who are around you. This results in you being in a positive and positive environment.

TEACH OTHERS

Another method to foster positive attitudes in yourself is to pass on that to others. A few of the strategies you're starting with can be very useful to your children should they adopt these techniques early on in their lives, before their minds are glued towards negative thinking. Consider how much easier life will be for them when they start as positive thinkers with an image of themselves that is positive from a young age. When you are known for having a positive personality, people will ask your how you constantly see things in a different way to other people. You will be able drop certain techniques that you've been learning from this site. Teaching them will not only increase your standing but also increase the positive image you want to embed into your personality.

Look for opportunities to be Grateful

Positive and gratitude are two different sides of the coin. It's nearly impossible to be thankful for anything without also being optimistic about it. Your day has started with a positive note. Look for little things to be grateful for throughout your day. As your mind adjusts to this new approach to thinking and being thankful for what you have will be a natural habit. Your eyes will suddenly open to a new world that has always been there however your senses have been conditioned to. The ability to appreciate them and dwell on them for a moment is among the most rewarding things you'll ever be able to do.

The physical BENEFITS

We've seen how our minds can exert positive influence on our bodies regards to overall health. Since the body and mind are so interconnected, there are many things we can physically do that affect our mental state. The act of getting up at a half hour earlier every day can have a profound impact on your mood and the amount you do. Of course, there are some who do not like mornings and the thought of being required to wake up earlier could send a chill through their spines. I am of the opinion that getting physically up from the bed is a result of our mental outlook on it which is the reason I've waited until near the close of the book to bring the subject up.

When your thoughts become more positive, you will notice that you view things differently than the way you did in the past. You'll start to see the positives even in the simplest things such as rising earlier. Similar is the case regarding exercise and eating a healthy diet. When you are focused on the positive, the relationship between mind and body will become clearer and you'll start to make more conscious choices regarding the way you take care of your body. This article is not meant to encourage a radical overhaul of your life, however, you must be aware of, and anticipate the possibility that resetting your mind can lead to shifts across the entirety of your life. Like me, you could start to alter the content you fill your mind. I'm often turned off by books and TV programs that I see as depicting negative issues. It wasn't my intention to make changes in these areas. It has just been a result of an improved outlook. The changes I've implemented to my eating and exercise routines have taken minimal effort. These are simply sensible changes that naturally occurred as a an outcome of thinking of the positive effects that these changes could bring.

"Positive thinking" is more than simply a slogan. It alters the way we act. I am convinced that when I'm positive that it does not just make me more effective, but it helps make the people who surround me better."

Harvey Mackay.

Chapter 7: How Emotional Intelligence Enhances Your Self-Confidence

Self-confidence is an attitude. It's a positive and healthy attitude towards your Self dimension. Self-confidence is not something you can learn by following the rules of a book; however, it can be nurtured and developed. It's a result of confidence and a sense of wellbeing. in your abilities in your abilities, knowledge and skills. It is not a result of arrogance or pride.

It's just an humble acknowledgement and acceptance of our inherent abilities and abilities, that is based on valuing and affirming these capabilities. Self-confidence is developed by regular practice, a the desire to gain more knowledge and positive thoughts, as well as training and self-acceptance.

If you're not confident as leader, you won't be able to make an effect on your followers, and might find it difficult to achieve success.

People who are confident face challenges and achieve success by having a confidence, which allows them to keep pushing forward to conquer the obstacles, those with low confidence in themselves, might not be brave enough to start the project, without persevering against the odds.

To ensure you display confident self-esteem, evaluate yourself with honesty and pay attention to your emotions as you respond to these questions.

Do I ever feel like I have all the solutions?

How can I handle criticism?

Do I usually make a statement in relation to certain issues?

Have I spent more time talking rather than listening?

Do I feel that there's an urge to display my pride and make others feel bad instead of being mindful of other peoples's views?

If you answered "yes" to one of these questions, you should learn to manage your emotions according to your self-confidence. Also, be prepared to be vulnerable. You must now begin detaching yourself from beliefs that you have to have the perfect answer each time.

Leadership transformation requires real confidence, which aids in balancing their requirements alongside those of their fellow team members.

Low confidence and overconfidence

Low confidence

Insecureness is a result of low self-esteem. It is due to a low self-esteem, insufficient confidence in one's abilities, or individual skills. People who aren't confident cannot display charisma, present themselves in a professional manner or even inspire others. They aren't suited to be leaders because they tend to be shy and aren't capable of speaking up with conviction and assertiveness. A lack of confidence can affect the effectiveness of the job and results in unmotivated leaders who pull team members along instead of inspiring them to be more effective.

Overconfidence

Arrogance is a result of overconfidence, and can be seen in some or all of these traits including a lack of willingness to apologize when you're wrong or being extremely defensive, not being able to admit fault and blustering.

When leaders make a mistake in judging their skills, knowledge and capabilities in a way that results in resentment from other people or appear domineering and unaware of how their decisions impact other people; this could be the result of confidence overconfidence. Overconfidence can be destructive and is not appropriate in the modern workplace. People who are too confident are unlikely to listen to advice from their team members or ask for assistance because they think they know all the answers.

Self-confidence that is tempered and level-headed is usually carried with modesty and humility excessive confidence can lead to inaccurate assessment, unrealistic expectations, and uncertain choices.

Chapter 8: How What You Can Do to Help Make a Difference

How do we begin making these modifications? The first step in helping you manage the stress ball, is to control those stress levels. In order to do this, you must return to the basics of humans.

The MASLOW pyramid is a basic structure that outlines the essential elements everyone needs. This simplified version divides the framework into three main sections.

Essential needs are those that we require to function, like sleeping, food shelter, security and food. They are also the most important of the base layers.

Psychological needs follow. They comprise friendships, relationships along with self-esteem, self-confidence respect and success.

Self-fulfillment must be at the top of the list and represents the process of becoming the best version of ourselves or achieving our maximum potential. This is a matter of morality, creativity and problem-solving.

Another example that is common is to divide human requirements into four parts that are known as:

Our skin, and everything else beneath, nourishment physical and healing.

Mental - perception, intellect thoughts, process of processing information.

Spiritual - connection with the self, others , and everything as well as guidance and protection.

The nervous system is responsible for emotions hormones, our emotions and relationships.

"Develop all four intelligences. "PQ (physical intelligence) which is comprised of 70 trillion cells that fight off disease and digest breakfast. The IQ (intellectual intelligence) and intelligence (emotional intelligence) the ability to sense and discern of the heart along with the SQ (spiritual intelligence) that deal with the meaning, purpose and integrity within your value system and your cherished source. When they're combined, they transform the world around us for good"

- Stephen Covey

It might appear like a lot of work to keep in check, but we're able to manage many of the four aspects in our lives as we move from childhood to adulthood. Most likely, the element that requires some effort is the ability to recognize indicators that indicate the area are being neglected and what you can do about it.

The following activities are ones which will give your mind the space to examine your own self objectively and identify areas that need focus.

Exercises to breathe

Find a place that you can comfortably sit for a couple of minutes. Relax your hands on your knees or in your lap and shut your eyes. Focus your attention on your breathing as you feel natural movements of your stomach and chest while your breath in and out. If your thoughts begin to move, acknowledge them, and let them go.

Inhale for 3 times and breathe in until two counts and out until 4 in the count. Next, take 3 breaths taking in 3 breaths and out for 4. Take three breaths by breathing in to the number of 4 and breathing out for four.

Allow your breath to fall in its own rhythm, and take a moment to rest. Your neck should be moved in the direction of a soft stretch and then take a moment to open your eyes.

The process of let go of thoughts is one which is personal to you. Instead of trying to stop your thoughts during the exercise, and then let them keep coming into your brain you can acknowledge the thought by saying , 'okay and that it's there'. Let the thought go by imagining that it is floating into a bubble or in a boat, and refocus in your breathing.

Stand and Stretch

Lift your arms over your head to create an upward stretch. Try to slow down your breathing to a normal pace, should it help you breathing in and out until three times.

Your head will move slowly in a circular motion in order to increase the length of your neck. Reduce your arms and then move your shoulders forward and reverse them.

Then bend forwards until you can feel your hands reaching your ankles or as high as you feel an increase at the back of your legs. Straighten your legs gently to increase the strength of the stretch. Relax your knees and then roll them back up and imagine the bones of your spine placing one on top of one as you move. Relax your arms by your sides, and take an inhale and out.

This basic stretch is perfect to let your frustration go or taking a breather during the computer all day. The goal of both stretching and breathing is to shift your focus off of a particular circumstance for a short period of time. You'll be amazed by the differences.

Other ways to investigate

Mindfulness is a practice so extensive that many people consider it to be a lifetime learning experience. Mindfulness comes in many forms however, the end goal is the identical. Mindfulness lets you step back from the situation and to be aware of the emotions you may be feeling and let them go so that you can view issues in a more rational manner. The recognition of feeling the way you do without judging your feelings is enough. A couple of seconds can be enough time to set off the emotional reaction. The intellectual section of your mind begins to whirl around and logic is able to take over from the knee-jerk reaction.

Reframing - changing negative thoughts thoughts into positive ones.

It's not possible to go to thinking that something's terrible to believing it's amazing, it's too much to be achieved all at once. The best thing we could do is slowly shift our thoughts in tiny steps, shifting from neutral to negative, then positive.

The purpose of being neutral is that you see things in a more realistic way and make the thought process much more manageable and lessening some of the expectations on yourself. This will allow you to make the quick switch from negative positive.

Our bodies and minds react to repeated actions. Our brains are filled with neural pathways that have been forged by experience and the actions we've repeated. The more you do and practice, the stronger the pathways get.

An excellent idea is to imagine writing using the opposite hand as regular. When you first write I'm almost certain that it will appear like an untrained toddler's handwriting.

If you go away and return then you'll desire to write using the normal hand once again. This is due to repetitive muscle thought processes. However, if you keep practicing with the other hand, your handwriting will improve because the pattern will become more well-known and the handwriting will improve gradually until it is natural. Even If you were to do it write with both hands and get flawless scriptive handwriting. It will take time, but keep your eyes on the ball and you'll continue to improve.

Write down the three or four negative thoughts you are thinking concerning yourself. What is an acceptable thought to focus on instead?

Negative Neutral

My stomach is like it's a bit bloated and wobbly. an human stomach

I'm having a very bad day at work. How do I be able to get through this? The day hasn't been great. How can I ensure tomorrow will be a better day?

I'm exhausted every day. It's possible that something is wrong within me. I'm tired more than normal. I'm planning to take an extended bath and then get an early start this evening.

The basics of taking care of

Feed your brain. Yes in terms of physical sensation. An increasing amount of research is proving the validity of the interconnectedness of our body and mind connections. Stress manifests as physical symptoms in more than three quarters of people suffering from it including headaches as well as high blood pressure and sleep disorders topping the list.

Your brain is a part of your physical self but it's often forgotten that in order to function properly, the brain needs a nutritious diet as does every other body part. The brain's primary energy source is protein , along with minerals and vitamins, so one of the most simple actions you can take is to ensure that your diet is high in these nutrients.

For those who eat meat, this means eating fish, meat dairy, leafy green vegetables. Vegans and vegetarians should ensure you have an adequate amount of beans, nuts, and pulses into your daily meals.

Hydration is also vital to brain function so make sure you drink plenty of regular water throughout the day and enjoy the benefits.

Physical fitness is generally accepted that moving is crucial to a healthy body, and not just for our muscles, digestion, and blood circulation. Regular exercise also helps to boost neuronal health by providing the healthy flow of nutrients and oxygen within the bloodstream, which can boost neuronal growth and connectivity in the brain.

Do you remember our Hippocampus?

It is becoming clear that exercise boosts neurogenesis (the formation in the development of new neural cells) within the hippocampal region which increases the capacity of emotion regulation as well as memory and learning in this important area.

With increasing evidence suggesting that many mental health issues like anxiety and depression are related to decreased hippocampal function, the importance of exercise is increasing. It's true that they say: healthful body and a healthy mind. It's not to suggest that we should all go out and exercise all day long. Incorporating a moderate quantity of fitness into your daily routine will be better than an occasional hour-long session. It is essential to be consistent in order to reap getting the most advantages.

Sleep - While the connection to mental wellbeing and sleep isn't yet completely understood however, we recognize that sleeping in a disturbed state is not healthy for our brains. The type of sleep during which we dream which is also known as rapid eye movement is believed to boost emotional health, memory , and the ability to learn. It is also believed that disturbed sleep can affect our mental processes and emotional regulation. If we get enough rest we can make sure that your restorative time is maximized as well as providing us with ample brain power to get through the day.

Tips to get enough rest include:

Establishing a routine for bedtime - spending time in a quiet space or reading, taking an enjoyable bath, or meditating. These activities can assist in signalling to your body and your mind that it's time to fall asleep. Your schedule will be different for you. So, you can try some things and then make a plan that you like.

Your bedroom is a sanctuary. bedroom a relaxing space to relax with soft lighting, comfy bedding and less clutter.

A mid-night meal - Many have found that having a small snack can be helpful however, others don't.

Relaxation time could include meditating, daydreaming or listening to audiobooks. The goal is to allow yourself a couple of minutes during which your brain is able to switch off from the daily grind.

All self-care and emotional intelligence practices are a continuous process. They require time to master and practice. The more you do, the more you'll gain.

"Empathy is the most important element that builds compassion. We must be able to recognize the things that another person goes through, how they're feeling and to incite compassion in us"

- Daniel Goleman

Empathy and Social Awareness is the ability to comprehend the needs of people who are around you, as well as the ability to recognize the feelings of others (empathy).

Social media and digital communication require some explanation as research shows that we're less empathic nowadays than some years ago. The result from this can be that we're less trustworthy, which is not ideal for personal or business relationships. When we demonstrate our awareness of the needs of another and show respect for the feelings of others, we earn their confidence. When we build trust, we can build credibility and establish positive connections.

Be attentive to the other person and be attentive to others. Time is our most precious resource and the majority of people appreciate having someone's complete attention even for a few minutes so turn off the phone.

Learn from other people by watching their actions and storing the notes in your mind to be ready for the next time. What are they doing differently? Did their approach work?

We all have different emotional states and coping capabilities. If you're not sure of how to interact with someone you know, take note of how they're reacting to other people and the language they're using. You can then alter your approach and your sensitivity according to.

The interpersonal skills we employ to interact with other people.

We are not all born with these abilities they are acquired and developed through repetition and making mistakes. Effective communication is essential to any relationship , and just like the ability to empathize, communication abilities are constantly being refined through the growing utilization of technology.

The improvement of interpersonal skills is equally important to ensure that your messages are delivered effectively and without creating conflicts. Self-management methods can assist us by ensuring that we make the necessary adjustments while trying to figure out how we can effectively manage our emotions.

Think about your non-verbal communication. the appearance of your clothes as well as body language and facial expressions all play a role in the non-verbal message you are sending out. Determine how you would like to be perceived and then make steps to achieve this appearance.

Accept responsibility and accountability of your choices. If you commit a blunder admitting it and apologizing can boost your credibility.

A positive attitude can help you seem more approachable to other people. Being positive and positive will assist you just as the other. Sharing a smile during work is an simple method to maintain a positive relationship between coworkers. The use of p's and Q's are another simple sign of respect that people truly appreciate. You should keep complaining to a minimum. Do you prefer to take a bite of something with a happy person, or one who is grumpy?

By paying attention to other people, you show them that you are interested. Listen to what they have to say and offer help when you can.

Keep shining - Your unique personality is important. While society can dictate certain manners of conduct, like politeness along with general high-level consideration. But it's possible to be over-emphasized and could lead to an era of robot-like humans.

Chapter 9: Reacting will lead to the same Results. Pausing will let You Pick Your Response

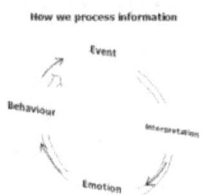

My friend rang from the phone to talk to her daughter. She seemed a bit worried. I asked her about the issue. She explained that her daughter handed her resignation to her employer because she wasn't getting along with her boss. I could tell she was concerned. I tried to soothe her by saying that If she really was dissatisfied and her boss didn't leave Maybe this was the best decision and surely a new position would appear in the near future?

Her main concern was not over the incident. It was happened to be the second job that her daughter quit in the span of two years and for the exact same reason. She was not a good fit with the boss. I have to admit it was a bit of a coincidence that she had three bosses that she did not connect with. In addition it would be lucky! My friend was concerned that it had nothing to do with have to do with her daughter's boss, but rather her daughter's reaction to a authoritative figure.

We begin to develop patterns of reacting which results in the same situations happening over and over again.

Everyone develops a habit of reacting to circumstances and even situations. There is a person I know who faced significant financial difficulties at a point in their life. However, they were able to overcome this and prospered afterward, when they were hit with an unexpected bill, they experienced a negative emotional reaction to the event. The negative feeling was tied to the fact that they had received an invoice even though they could easily pay for any expense and have become extremely wealthy.

There is a natural sequence of our actions. The below diagram illustrates the cycle or process that we are following. It is not always conscious and we are at an exact point in the process, without knowing what is happening.

Events evoke thought/interpretation

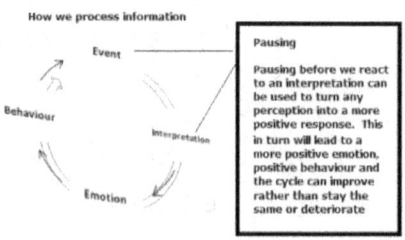

The way we think determines what our feelings are (emotions).

Our emotions influence our behavior.

We are thinking and we interpret the emotions we experience and the behavior we exhibit. This interpretation could add to any negative feelings or boost our joy if our perception is positive.

The way we react can affect our surroundings. Behaviours that are based on positive emotions can will result in happy, peaceful results. Behaviors that are triggered by negative emotions may result in a worsening of the circumstance or incident which is repeated.

To stop this cycle, it is necessary to be able to take a break in the stage of interpretation. For instance, a person who has financial difficulties be at the stage of interpretation, rather than thinking "Oh this is a bad old charge, if this goes on I could be in trouble once more" may think instead: " Another bill, how am I thankful that I have enough money to cover this quickly, am I fortunate? Or is it just luck?" Which would make you feel more at ease?

You're not going to win any prizes for guessing.

Below is a sketch of the theoretical model with a built-in timer at the stage of interpretation. Pause before reacting can be the very first stage in developing amazing emotional intelligence. This trick will show clearly to you that you can always alter your feelings about something, simply by creating a more positive thinking idea.

Refraining from reacting in the hope of creating a better thinking thought, is the first step in establishing your goal to always respond, not react positively. Reacting positively is always in line with our authentic self.

The process of achieving better-feeling thoughts and consequently feeling better is a process , and you must climb the emotional ladder by stepping up the ladder in phases

If you're in a dark state of emotional states, and are lost in negative thoughts for a long time, then it could take a while to get into a positive mindset and feeling more positive. Thinking and feeling better can be a gradual process. It can take couple of seconds, several days, or even months. It all depends on how firmly rooted or fixed your thought and beliefs are that can be the cause of the negative feelings.

This is what I refer to as "The emotional Climb" which is an emotional ladder. The ladder is a way to assess where we are and also as a means to feel better, when we're committed to aligning with our authentic self.

Let's take a look at the steps of how the ladder might be utilized.

John took PS1000 from the banking institution to purchase a second-hand automobile. The owner of the car had demanded on cash. When he returned back to the bank, John was unable to locate his purse and the money inside. Even after doing everything he could to find it, retracing his steps, making contact with authorities, it was as if the wallet had disappeared for the last time. The man was devastated. Everyone could be. It's extremely challenging to John not to feel optimistic regarding such an incident.

What we've been taught to do is reflect on the incident. In this instance, John was clearly contemplating the possibility of losing money. His mood was fluctuating between the steps 9 and 12. He felt depressed and down felt guilty and blamed himself. He was angry.

If he kept thinking about the possibility of losing his money and he did not change his mind about the issue, it is possible that he'll get stuck in a spiral of despair, blameing himself in anger and full of blame.

Over time, he may eventually, he'll find himself repressing his thoughts and feelings, or simply "forgetting" about the loss of money to get some relief from negative thoughts and feelings. The issue with this method is that each time someone remembers that he lost the money, he will immediately be back in his negative mood.

If, on the other hand, he determined that he really wanted to be more content with losing the cash, then the way to resolving his feelings about this incident could be his primary plan.

So he could tell him: "This is an awful loss, but, you have to remember that sometimes bad things happen and even people make mistakes". Then he could take one step higher. He could then think. In reality, it was an extremely devastating error and I'm really fortunate, I have a loving and spouse who is supportive, and two beautiful children, I'm going to put this incident in the context of how lucky that I am". He then climbs another step up the ladder.

If John was experiencing the full impact of his negative thoughts it is likely (without some training) that he'd be able to climb from the lowest rungs to Step 1 which brings happiness, love and inspiration in a short time. If he was willing to let go of his negative thoughts and feel about losing the money instead of burying or suppressing the thoughts and feelings he has about it, he could really put the entire incident in the proper perspective and not let it be a source of worry for him.

I want to emphasize that at this point that if you or anyone else is thinking or being extremely negative about an event, it is important to be aware that your feelings are legitimate! What you feel is a result of your thoughts, beliefs , and thoughts about the issue. When you are able to fully embrace your feelings, you can decide to keep the thoughts, beliefs and emotions that can make you feel negative or overcome your negative thoughts, beliefs and emotions, that will bring you back in alignment with your authentic self. It's your choice. Be aware that all your feelings are gifts regardless of whether they are negative or not since they can provide useful information about whether or not you're in alignment with your inner self or not.

To develop emotional intelligence, we can get our minds off of the cycle and experience an easier to feel thought. If you regularly practice this and consistently, you'll build an individual ladder climbing towards more pleasant thoughts that bring you into the right place with your inner self. It takes some discipline and practice however it leads us to the second secret in which detachment plays the secret to a strong connection.

Chapter 10: Relevance of Self-Awareness

Introspection, or becoming conscious of oneself, refers to knowing your needs, desires as well as your habits, weaknesses and all the other aspects that make you the person you are. The more you are aware of yourself, the better you can manage yourself to improve your life. For example those who know the way they get distracted by their smartphone when they work could implement strategies to minimize the distractions of technology in order to be more efficient. In the absence of being aware of the problem you can't implement strategies to improve it.

Self-awareness is an integral part of both psychology and philosophy. Socrates once wrote, "Know thyself." Though it could be a shock that self-awareness goes beyond simply self-examination at one level. You need to be aware of your feelings, too.

If you pay more focus on your emotions and how they function more you'll be able to understand the reasons behind the things you do. The more you understand about your habits and habits, the easier it will be to change the habits you've developed. In the majority of cases it will require some time and effort.

You can study every tip for productivity that is available on the internet, take on the habits of some people who are among the top individuals on the planet and read through every bit of self-help info available but the point is in the absence of knowing how you can improve on yourself to put the best suggestions into action.

As an example, Joe is an entrepreneur who rises early at 5 a.m. each day to shower, make his breakfast, and head to work at 7 a.m. Every day Joe is tired unhappy, angry, and generally not productive at work. He is tempted to go to bed earlier and increasing his intake of caffeine in the morning and even attempts to nap during the afternoon. But nothing seems to work.

The freelancer is still not productive and his freelance work is beginning to fall.

Then, Joe has a breakdown and sleeps till 9 a.m. and then is awake feeling refreshed and refreshed. He is able to finish more work and has deeper connections with his clients and has more time to focus on a pastime that he's always wanted to pursue. He's often up all night until eleven a.m. at night and then when he is asleep, he's more productive than since he began his freelancing business.

The next day, Joe wakes up at 9 a.m. and not five. The day is as productive as the previous one and he's feeling more confident about himself. At this point, that Joe realizes that he's not an early riser He's a night-owl and is more productive when he is following the internal clock.

Self-awareness may not be the solution to productivity or emotional intelligence, however this is the initial step and emotional intelligence can't happen without it.

It's quite easy to be sucked into the notion that if you are aware of yourself and are in a position to make everything better but that's not the way it operates. Human brains are packed with biases that guide our choices. Being more conscious of your own needs and your needs will aid you in your journey to the essential elements of emotional intelligence.

Chapter 11: The Way to Be Emotionally Intelligent

The concept of emotional intelligence, as discussed in previous chapters, refers to the capability to comprehend and manage your personal feelings while also recognizing and managing the emotions of other people. It's been scientifically proven that people who have a greater EQ achieve better results at work than people with a higher IQ. The ability to be emotionally intelligent is a greater ability when it comes to making decisions and listening to other people as well as helping others, showing compassion and so on. It is apparent that just having an IQ that is high IQ and low or no EQ isn't enough to succeed in any field, not just at work , but all around.

This chapter will concentrate on teaching you how to become emotionally smart.

Psychologists frequently inquire about how their patients feel. This isn't an ordinary question, it's an important one that's more profound than people imagine it is. The way you feel and the ability to acknowledge emotions is the most important element from which anyone can begin to understand their feelings and becoming (even) more emotionally knowledgeable.

Begin by acknowledging your emotions as not just bad or good and as a source of data that will allow you to be more aware and conscious. A lot of people, if not everyone, have thought of emotions as something negative as something that holds us back, and doesn't assist us in all areas that we are involved in. The most difficult part of being an emotionally intelligent person is ignoring the fact that emotions are either good or bad. They exist to can aid us and provide us a glimpse into our personality as well as how we respond in certain circumstances, and the things we can do to control our emotions.

Let's look at ways to enhance your emotional intelligence

1. Reducing negative emotions.

We begin with negative emotions because we have a tendency to "jump" into them. If you wish to alter the way you feel about an event then you need to alter your perception of it. Start by cutting down on personalization that is negative. What is that? Negative personalization refers to the feeling of negativity you feel regarding the behavior of another. The easiest method to achieve this is to avoid to conclude that the person you are talking to is ignorant, stupid or lazy. or whatever. In this case instead of jumping into the idea that your friend didn't call you back due to cheating, you should consider the possibility that they're distracted or may be sleeping, or that they cannot hear their phone and so on. The less you focus on others' behavior and actions, the better you will be able to observe their actions. It is important to realize that people's actions are always focused on them, not necessarily about you.

2. Reduce stress, stay cool.

It sounds simple but in actuality there are people who do the opposite. We live in a society where the more busy we are the better we believe we're doing. The more stressful our lives are and the more successful we believe we're. It's hard to convey that a person who's busy isn't always a successful one. Stress isn't completely avoided because of the way this world works but how we deal with stressful situations can make us more assertive or reacting. Every person will be in a stressful circumstance at some point in their life. If you're experiencing stress it is important to stay cool and keep your head at ease. Anxiety or nervousness can cause an adverse effect on your whole body (some people feel it in their digestive tract while others suffer from headaches and so on.). It's no surprise that you require cooling air when things get hot. This isn't just a flimsy suggestion as lower temperatures actually lower anxiety.

Coffee and other beverages cause anxiety
If you are aware that your workday is likely

to be stressful, make sure you don't drink too much coffee.

If you feel down, depressed and are constantly afraid should consider doing exercise aerobically. The more cardio you perform and the more relaxed your body will feel afterwards. The old saying that motion is the determinant of emotions is an excellent illustration of this. Exercise can also increase dopamine levels which makes you feel more positive and healthier. As your body gets in better shape and your confidence grows.

3. Take care of those who are negative in your life. Get rid of the negative people in your.

Sometimes, we cannot keep these people out of our lives, regardless of how difficult we attempt. Many people are trapped in such relationships and relationships, regardless of whether it's by decision. Maybe you are dealing with a negative relationship or co-worker or even a family member who is negative. These people tend to be more dominant in their emotions. They are able to cause chaos in your life and cause you to be in a bad mood, or to even begin an dispute with you. Of course, this can affect your mood and you must be a good steward when managing these people.

Whatever the they are, or how difficult they are, ensure that you keep your cool and think about it before saying anything that will cause you to feel awful following the event. Reactivity should be reduced maybe by counting 10 times or taking some deep breaths or taking a break to take breath, or doing to be quiet. Try to imagine yourself in the shoes of your fellow citizens. Consider their lives, the things that make them feel so depressed or negative, etc. Do not let negative thoughts take over your thoughts. Instead, think about your options and realize that it should not be simple to them to behave in like they do.

Whatever you feel about how compassionate you might be, you must remember that their actions aren't something you have to accept. The most important point in this case is that people do act in a particular way due to their own personal issues. Most times there is no reason to blame. They express their frustration through their negative or difficult behavior to other people, too. In the end, day, these behaviors reveal much about the people involved in them, not you. Depersonalization is essential to be able to discern the situation in a clear way.

4. To name an emotion.

It's not uncommon for people to experience emotions but not be able to express it. In most cases people are able to name their emotions, however it's common for them to aren't willing to admit the feelings because of fear. When you name the emotion, especially in public it's not just that you become aware of your emotions, but you also create relationships between the thoughts you have and the way you feel. By doing this, you're actively reducing the gap between your unconscious and conscious states. In this way you don't just have the ability to manage and better understand your emotions but you're also moving forward in realizing what you're feeling. If you're feeling angry, speak the words loudly; there's no need for anyone else present. When you say it, be aware that you're angry and then acknowledge the reason you are feeling this way. If you're feeling happy, enthusiastic or thrilled, speak it loudly. Say something like "I'm looking forward to going to the beach" or "I'm happy to be watching this movie". You're developing a sense of your feelings, and by making a statement about it, you're becoming an emotionally aware person.

5. Be aware of the right time to stop.

You've decided to improve you emotional intelligence. This means that you'll need to be more contemplative conscious, aware, and self-aware However, this can be an extremely consuming process when your attention is solely on you. It's a great thing to be introspective however, you must be aware of the moment when you need to look around and take a step back. The ability to be emotionally intelligent isn't just about you, it's about others too. Be aware of your thoughts, but also try to comprehend the emotions of others. Focus on your own inner self, the way you feel and the way others are feeling and behave must be in perfectly balanced way.

What are the indicators to tell if you're making progress on your way to becoming an emotionally knowledgeable person? Yes, you can try these techniques, you'll be more conscious of the way you feel and identify your feelings, and depersonalize your behavior with others and so on. However, what's the final result?

You'll soon realize that you're fully conscious of how you feel. If you've always felt "good" and "bad" prior to now, you'll know exactly if you're anxious, angry or annoyed or content, inspired and excited, etc.

The evidence of emotional intelligence is your curiosity about people around you. An active curiosity (not just asking what they're doing in order to have small conversations) is an indication of empathy , and an excellent indicator of an EQ that is high. EQ.

You'll no longer be scared of changes. People are naturally scared of change, because they're scared of being in the dark. Change is the most devastating setback to the path to personal satisfaction and success. As your emotional intelligence improves you'll be more excited and eager to see the next chapter in your life without being compelled to harm yourself or remain at the same place that you were (both physically and in a metaphorical sense).

As an emotionally intelligent individual You'll be less easily offended. In addition, you'll be more open and capable of not focusing on the actions of others Additionally, you'll have a stronger skin which is a great quality. Being able to not be offended is a true superpower and you won't be spending time thinking about why someone was offended or what their motives were.

You'll be able to easily evaluate characters, you'll be able to discern the intentions of others and what they're thinking about and so on. This will result of your increased awareness of yourself and understanding that people act the way they do for themselves.

The greater your emotional intelligence will be, the more easily you'll be able to say "no. Notice how effortlessly you can will be able to say "no" without having to or desire to justify yourself as well as apologize. If you've in the past have said, "I won't be able to do this, I'm sorry" or "I don't think I'm going be able to make it this evening" Now, you'll not be required to say anything other than a simple "no". This indicates greater self-control. It's not easy but it's totally doable.

The ability to be emotionally intelligent will give you the desire to get rid of negativity, gossip and people who complain constantly. You'll be thankful for what you have. You'll be driven to care for and take care of yourself in any way you can by eating healthy meals to getting enough rest.

The final flourish will be the realization of the desire to attain perfection. People who are emotionally intelligent don't look for perfection since they realize it's not there. The pursuit of perfection is a long journey that can result in lots of discontent, anger, and stress. Think about whether you want to be constantly thinking about what you could accomplish to get an improved outcome or to feel elated to have got the result you wanted and you've done the best you could to reach the moment and where you are today.

Chapter 12: The Way Of Intimacy

Perhaps you're not worried about your work or you're at a job that you are happy in but the issue is that you're among the people who wish they had more communication with their partners. If you're one of them and your spouse is always irritated by your lack of memory or falling off, it might be one of the most troubling things that are happening within your daily life. However, don't worry about it because there's a method to correct that. The act of listening can transform your life and relationships , and this is how.

It fosters intimacy.

Simple. A relationship that is successful can't be measured in terms of time together, number of sex sessions or the degree of happiness you feel. A relationship that is successful is measured by the degree of intimacy attained through the relationship. What is the reason for intimacy? Because everything is connected to intimacy. Are you looking for more sexual pleasure? Get intimate. Are you looking to have a long-lasting marriage? Get intimate. Are you looking to be more happy and satisfied in your relationship? Get intimate. Intimacy is a sign that you're doing things right. We all know what intimacy means and, if not, you'll be able to recognize it once you experience it. It's the feeling of being one that connects souls, the desire to communicate even if it's for nothing, the desire to tear their clothes off, take in intimate moments as well as many other amazing moments. This all goes through the door of intimacy. How can you encourage more intimacy? What are the steps you can take to follow the path of intimacy?

I. Begin to actively listen:

Similar to the professional meeting the process begins with paying attention. Be aware that your partner, spouse or girlfriend/boyfriend want to feel valued by you. In order to prove that you are you're there, you have to be attentive in conversations. Ask questions, be supportive and give them the respect they deserve. If you're caught up in something that's important and want to share it with them, do it to ensure that they don't feel unimportant. Being attentive to the person you cherish will let them know that you're important to me. It's a method of drawing people closer and it's sincere.

II. the Art of Anticipation:

Understanding what's essential to your loved one, it's not going to simply happen. You can't take in their struggles concerns, fears dreams, love, and worries simply by being there with them. You can only gain these insights through listening to them, and it helps you recognize when something important happens in their lives or there's something troubling in the near future It is possible to be supportive for them. This lets them know that you are aware of the current situation, you're concerned about their issues and are for them during the day-to-day events. Nobody wants to be left alone, and they cherish you, so take care to show them love.

III. Reciprocation encourages:

When you know that what they've shared with you, and what they've said towards you matters to them and your loved ones, they are encouraged to be closer to you, and to continue to invest in you. You'd like this because it's the basis of intimacy and it will show them how much you cherish them. So , if you want to encourage your beloved one to continue talking about their lives with you, listening to them and telling them that you're with them and you're with them will only increase the intimacy. Encourage them to continue sharing, and show them how much you appreciate them. The experience will only get better.

When you are pursuing the pursuit of intimacy Your relationships will appear like they're growing and more each day. You'll find out new information out about your most trusted partner and friend. You'll get to know the needs of them and anticipate their requirements. If you build and invest in your partner or spouse you will be a standout from the rest of them. They'll tell you they've only met one person ever met who really listened to them or could have understood their needs. It's a sad fact that they could be right. Show them respect and affection and let them know that you're not disposable. Show them that you truly cherish you and are a part of their lives. This will create the love needed for a long-lasting relationship.

Chapter 13: Develop People Skills

Being a good empath will not be of any benefit when you are unable to say correctly or take the correct actions. So, it is important to learn and keep enhancing your people capabilities.

People skills refers to the process of communicating, listening and connecting. It's a lot like the previous lesson. However, it is important to understand it is a sensory ability.

People aren't able to express what they feel, because they don't want to or simply aren't able to. When we look back at the example of lost baggage the passenger voiced displeasure instead of anger. He could have just stated "I am very upset by this tragic event, as all of my personal belongings are there. What can you do to assist me retrieve my belongings within the shortest time possible?" Instead, however he slammed his report with insults and criticisms in order to unleash his anger anger and to resist to do so. In this scenario, you'll require good senses to discern the anger. And that's the purpose of empathy.

People abilities On the other hand is more crucial in the sense that you're trying to view a particular situation from the perspective of someone else.

Listening

There are two kinds of listeners. The first listener is able to come up with a response while the other listens to learn. If you're looking to enhance social relationships then go with the second.

Responding to comments is often overloaded with judgment and self-esteem. The type of person who listens to reply fills the gaps by assuming facts or uses irrelevant information to show off his excellence. Listening to comprehend On the other hand is selfless because it is unabated If it is unclear, the listener seeks clarification.

While it sounds easy to listen but you'll be amazed at the difficulty. If you're not on the journey to mastering emotions, your uncontrolled mind will overflow your head with judgement. When you do recall your conversation will you realize that you I didn't really listen to comprehend.

Communication

People who are emotionally intelligent speak clearly. Whether they are aware whether or not they are aware when words are unclear and, if they do they are aware of how the person listening is likely to interpret their message. The ambiguity of the message can lead to multiple interpretations and, in the majority of cases it leaves two people confused.

It's not possible to convey your ideas in an exact manner since no two people have the exact same mindset. When people are processing information, they combine it with their personal experiences as well as their own understanding of the context in order to understand the message behind it, not really understanding what the other is really saying. An easy example is a funny joke. If the person who isn't have a clue about the context, he isn't able to understand the joke. If he knows the context but doesn't think it was funny, he's not got the experience and personal knowledge to appreciate the irony.

Relating

To relate is to look from the point of view of someone else. It differs from empathy in the sense that it isn't entirely emotional. It is simply understanding what the other person is getting their information from.

A friend's story of being fired from their job, for instance, even though you've never experienced it personally, is a matter of relating. It can be difficult to feel empathy in the absence of knowing exactly what it's like, more so if you realize it's not a good employee he believes himself to be. However, instead of creating a worse impression for your friend by pointing out his shortcomings instead, you acknowledge his circumstances by offering him a hug and a reassurance that you understand. When you say you understand you're saying that, even though you're not sure what it's like, getting removed from your job is a blow to the face and it is painful.

Level-headedness

It is perhaps the most crucial skill for people and is especially important for people who are working in stressful situations. Maintaining calm even when everyone else is frantic is not a common skill. In fact, NASA recognizes calmness in astronauts. They selected Neil Armstrong for the moon mission specifically due to the rare talent he has.

To be able to stay calm requires a complete understanding of one's emotions. Although it isn't easy doing this, it yields countless benefits , especially when it comes to improving relationships with others. One of the most desirable things people seek in other people is calmness, as it's contagious. There's plenty going on their heads and in their lives that an individual with a calm, peaceful state is an oasis of calm.

Lessons 4 and 5 go together in a lot of situations. For instance, how would you be sympathetic when you don't listen to the struggles of a person you know? Skills for people, however, can play a significant function in the professional setting. If you're not in the service sector there isn't a lot of workplaces that be a place where you can feel emotions with some exceptions. Most people keep their emotions locked up due to the need to remain professional. Of course, this can be risky and that's why you need to have a good interpersonal skill to break the barriers to gain confidence of your colleagues.

Exercise 5

Listening

Listening is the exercise identical to that to practice empathy. Engage with people and try your best to be attentive without making assumptions.

Communication

There isn't a magic formula to become well-read. Think, write, and think These three practices will eventually help you get there. However, to begin your daily practice, you should avoid using universal quantifiers, such as "any", "all" or "every" since they allow an open door for endless variations.

Relating

The only method of acquiring this ability is to talk to people , or at the very minimum being attentive to them. If you're in a position to do so you can join intervention programs or attending seminars on intervention. Take a look at the experiences of others and try to look at things from their perspective. You'll discover such things as certain addicts aren't in any way evil but simply human beings who are enduring similar struggles similar to yours.

Level-Headedness

The ability to remain composed and calm must be developed through consciously engaging in difficult situations and absorbing the lessons later. Gradually but carefully introduce pressure to your life by assuming the responsibilities. Instead of binge-watching Netflix in your home after work, you can volunteer for charities or take on freelance work when it is necessary to work with strangers.

The army can push recruits to the edge in order to build this capability. They are exhausted, starved and keep their minds alert. When their minds aren't working at its best they are forced to think of solutions for issues. The most difficult part is that they have to collaborate and coordinate with tired and angry comrades.

There's no need to go to war, therefore exposing yourself to these extremes isn't required. But it does open you up to the possibility that regardless of how much you've progressed in controlling your emotions, it's all can go to waste when you get overwhelmed or lose control in situations of extreme stress.

Chapter 14: Proud to be authentic

I recall someone saying that they weren't happy with me about something. I considered it for a while before I realized that, when it came to my personal lives were concerned, my opinions were legitimate. I'm the first to listen to criticism and utilize it to make improvements in myself, yet fundamentally everyone has a unique aspect to them, particularly those with emotional intelligence. They'll be able to agree on differences and appreciate the fact that opinions of others matter in the same way that their opinions are important to their own credibility.

If you dress the way you do in order to be in line with certain guidelines, do you feel comfortable with your clothes? If yes, then you're authentic. Have you ever seen someone wearing fashionable clothes but isn't comfortable in the clothes? I'm sure that people who wobble in high-heeled footwear are not authentic. They're trying to be conformist to standards that they believe are superior to their own. Do you remember hearing of someone trying to talk about themselves, only to stumble because they're not being themselves? They're trying to use phrases and words that will delight their viewers.

Are you authentic? It is important to examine the aspects of your life that are important. The people that are significant in your life appreciate your character as who you are. People who aren't particularly fond of your personality shouldn't be attracted to admiring you just because you perform. This isn't authentic, and the people you're trying to impress don't want to know your real personality because they've not had the pleasure of seeing it. When meeting new individuals, you strive to present the best version of yourself. But what you show at times is that you transform into a persona that does not make mistakes or fits the mold. Let me explain. If you took a picture from

Mona Lisa Mona Lisa and placed it in a frame made of plastic red, it'd look strange. It would not be authentic and could be considered an error of judgment. In the event that you place an image of the Mona Lisa into a traditional frame, people would accept it and even praise it since it's consistent with what is the Mona Lisa is. It is important to present yourself in the way you want to be and not what you imagine other people want to be portrayed for you to become the person you are in your truest form.

It's a brief section, yet it can teach you a great deal about emotional intelligence. Examine the way you act when you are in the presence of others. Are you authentic? Do people believe that you are who you claim to be? If you can believe in yourself, other things follow. It is important to reach the point at which you feel confident in who you are If you are looking to increase the level of your performance in terms of emotional intelligence. There's no pretense. There is no pretext. However, there is the ability to be attentive, the ability to act in a responsible way in the face of circumstances, and to be content with the way you respond to the world. If you're not, there is some work to do in order to achieve that goal, however, when you examine your relationships with other people they can provide you with plenty of clues. If, for instance, you do not get along with anyone, why? Find out the reason and explain them well enough so that you are confident in your choice. It's possible to find that being authentic can be more difficult than you imagine but it's worthwhile. People will admire the person you are and will be able to trust you since they are aware of where they stand. If you encounter something that makes you feel uncomfortable take the time to explore it so that you can improve your character and be prepared to face any circumstance regardless of how uncomfortable they have made you previously. This is your opportunity to shine.

Chapter 15: Establish Accountability

The entire concept of emotional intelligence could be summarized in one word: control. The people who are not emotionally intelligent are those who have no the ability to control their emotions health as well as their thoughts, their words, and the way they behave. In the end, instead of being in control of their emotions, they allow their emotions take control of them. People who have developed emotional intelligence are in control of their emotions, and consequently controlling their words, thoughts and actions. These people are not just in control of their behavior and reactions however, more often than not they also determine the course of occasions they're involved in. This leads to a greater sense control over the events of life.

To achieve the level of self-control, a person needs to learn to take responsibility for their actions. Only when you are held to account for what you do can you be in complete the control of them. When you refuse to take accountability for your words or actions, you let these elements influence you, and rather than the other way around. It is therefore crucial to develop a mindset that is accountable, rather than one that doesn't. In addition, by creating an attitude of self-accountability, you can help others be more accountable, thus increasing the impact of emotional intelligence across all who are involved.

Always admit your mistakes

The most important principle of accountability is that you admit your faults. This is the primary way that most people become unable to manage their lives. If you don't accept your responsibility for making mistakes you'll never be able to be able to learn from the mistakes that will enable you avoid repeating the same mistakes again. This means that you'll remain to consider, talk, and behave in ways that can could lead to failure, rather than success. And, even more importantly, when you run away from your mistakes, you let the fear of failing to set in and dictate your way of thinking. This is why many people feel the fear of failure and the reason why so many tend to make the same mistakes repeatedly.

Most successful individuals understand that everyone is prone to making mistakes. This is why they don't judge other people based on their mistakes and instead judge them by the way they learn from their mistakes. This is a indicator of emotional as well as mental power. If you acknowledge your mistakes, you show the courage that others aren't able to display. So, even if your situation may not be ideal your character is seen as strong and positive. At the end of the day this will contribute to establish your image within the workplace for being brave confident, reliable and able to overcome challenges. It is obvious that having a good reputation can help you achieve the highest degree of success, regardless of the place you are employed.

Another reason that admitting your mistakes can increase emotional wisdom is that it stops blame-shifting to other people. You will often see individuals who are quick to blame others when things get out of hand. If things are going well they'll be the first person to sign their name to the line. When mistakes happen or setbacks happen this is when they let others be the center of attention. This can ruin an individual's reputation since it puts them into the category of people who would put you under the to the curb. They aren't a person to be trusted and are always treated with disdain. So when you establish accountability, you eventually establish confidence.

Embrace imperfection

If you acknowledge your mistakes and accept responsibility, you are accountable in the aftermath, which means that you take responsibility for your actions following events that changed in the wrong direction. There is a method to establish accountability prior to even taking the situation into consideration this ensures that you take responsibility for the event from beginning to end. This is by accepting imperfections. If you accept imperfection you anticipate the possibility that mistakes will occur and setbacks are likely to occur. Then, you accept responsibility for any outcome that could occur, even before they happen. This is the real meaning of having complete control of the situation you find yourself in.

One of the biggest benefits of accepting imperfections is that it reduces the fear of failing. Failure is only viewed as a negative thing in the event that you want not to fail at any cost. If you view setbacks and mistakes as normal parts of every endeavor, you'll reduce the anxiety they cause. Additionally, as well as stopping fear, this method will help you let your mind be open to the lessons that could be learned from mistakes when they fail. The truth is that you may need to find out what's not working before you discover the things that work. It is possible to achieve this by deciding to accept the flaws of every plan, effort or aim.

Accepting the imperfections of life is the best way to build emotional intelligence in other people as well. If you can assure others that mistakes are an integral element of life, they'll be less self-conscious about making mistakes, and thus eliminate the shame and fear that mistakes can create. In addition, by removing the guilt and shame from making mistakes foster a sense of integrity in your colleagues. If people aren't scared to admit their mistakes, they'll be less likely to attempt to cover them. Instead, they'll be keen to discover a solution so they can rectify the errors and move on. That is how success will ever be attained within the work place. If people are trying to blame others for their mistakes or conceal the mistakes they make, the situation can only get worse to worse. But, if everyone is honest and transparent about the entire project, they are able to attain an outcome every single time. It's merely a matter of being in control of the situation, rather than making the situation take over you.

Chapter 16: Building emotionally Effective Relationships

The ability to manage the emotions of people around you is among the most important abilities we can develop in the current frenzied world of social media. How many times have people get angry or defensive after you've said something that is unflattering or offensive to them? We've had a hard time keeping track. The way they react defines their emotional intelligence. However, your ability to manage these emotions and channel them in a positive way determines your own.

Imagine how many instances you've felt frustrated and angry with people for not completing an obligation they've been given within the deadlines they were given (both professionally and personally). They get more defensive and anxious when you inquire about your request. If you're not a great performer in emotions, then you'll wind feeling frustrated, and offending the other party. The second issue is that the job to be completed will remain incomplete.

A person who is emotionally intelligent can determine the reasons behind an individual's lack of motivation or interested in the work. They could offer an additional aid to the person in need or put in an incentive to inspire them.

The strong emotions that we experience are the result of someone's values being infringed upon. If we violate something that is of tremendous significance or value to someoneelse, the person's reaction is a kind of external expression of a negative perception of the situation.

There isn't a special scan using x-rays that allows us to discover the thought processes that led to these negative emotions. We can't get into the minds of people to discover why they're angry. We are only able to observe the emotional reaction , without being aware of the triggers. With such a limited understanding of the thought processes that trigger the expression of an emotion, how can you handle the emotions of others in your vicinity?

Here are some excellent tips to help navigate the treacherous river of people's emotions and emotions in stressful and stressful situations, and more effectively manage them.

Pay attention to the behavior of people
The issue isn't just about paying attention to the words people speak. It's about more than just their words to detect non-verbal and verbal clues such as voice tone as well as gestures, body language and expressions. Be aware of people's behavior to detect subtle signals about their feelings from their inner world.

Pay attention to your actions by asking yourself questions such as - Do they have their voice fluctuate? What are their hands' positions? Are they to pink whenever they talk? Are they keeping eye contact with you consistently or is their gaze shifting often? Are they getting more assertive and aggressive during conversations? Being aware of these subtle but important signs can offer you a wealth of information regarding their feelings. This will help you manage the situation and handle it better before it gets out of control. It's a bit difficult to be an active participant as well as an observer during a conversation, but it is possible to master this skill through practice.

Don't try to match their Intensity What number of times have you been in a position to look for an eye, and then shout at double the decibels the other person has thrown at us? The truth is that emotionally intelligent people do not believe in comparing the intensity of the other. They know that this could only escalate an otherwise manageable issue.

If temperatures are high It is important to remain keep your cool and be able to think in a rational manner. It's an emotional race where you need to defeat your adversary. If you have escaped reason through the door of another person then invite it into your house. Think logically and try managing your emotional reaction to an impulsive emotion. Keep calm, rational and calm. Try to manage the potentially explosive situation by arguing and discussing the situation with your partner.

Utilize more reflection statements Reflection statements help people to view their situation from your perspective. It also communicates your brain that you're trying to comprehend their emotions and actions. Reflecting on statements can help reduce the tension in a potentially explosive situation since it reduces the emotional response of the other party. It's also possible to concentrate on their actions and behavior instead of just their words.

For example, it's evident that you're angry about something. I've noticed you saying these (their word choice) or noticed that over the past couple of days, you've spoken less in meeting of the team (their actions) Is there something that you're unhappy about?

Finish with Questions: Make a thoughtful statement , and then follow it with a short question to assist in getting the meaning behind the emotion that is hidden. For instance, you might use the phrase, "I notice you're upset. What's happening? When you observe their actions or their emotions explore the deeper meaning behind their reactions by asking them questions.

Sometimes looking for hidden, deeper meanings can provide us with amazing understanding of a person's behavior and makes it much easier for us to handle our own and that of the behavior of the other person.

If a person is becoming increasingly emotional during a particular situation, one of most effective ways to help them to think rationally is to ask a variety of questions. This aids in gradually shifting them from the emotional brain and into the brain's logical function center.

The more sophisticated questions you ask the more likely they'll reduce their emotional intensity. You can ask more rational questions for successfully restoring your logic.

Change the setting or activity If someone is becoming more aggressive, defensive or experiencing other negative emotions Try to get them to engage in physical exercise. Try going up and down steps, go for an exercise, go for the run, or find a quiet space to talk. Changes in the physical environment often alters the brain's electrical circuits in order to let them disconnect from the demands that are placed on their brains by their physical activities.

Allow them to share their story Let them share their story: Be compassionate towards people who are in difficult circumstances through asking them tell their perspective or story about the situation. Sometimes, you'll gain an completely new perspectives (which you had not even thought of) and enable you to understand the person more. Pay attention to them with a keen eye and in a non-judgmental way.

Get an understanding of the things they wanted but were unable to achieve. Ask them if you have unknowingly breached their wishes and expectations.

If you're a leader or manager in the right direction, you'll find that a majority of your team members or subordinates are in a bad mood or disagreements, and they have really bad days. The way you handle them at this point determines your emotional level. It will reveal how well you are aware of their feelings and emotions.

Instead of pretending there's no problem, or more shaming or blaming those who are acting out Try to provide them with the opportunity to talk and express their emotions. The ability to empathize, be compassionate, and understanding are all obvious indicators of a well-developed emotional intelligence.

If the negative behavior is a pattern of conduct within the workplace, employees may require assistance from a specialist by way of counseling to pinpoint the root cause.

Know What They Really Value Find out all the emotions that lie beneath an individual by simply asking them what their goals and aspirations are. Ask them to explain why they would like to tap further into their emotional well and discover their core values.

For instance, someone could claim that they want to make sure that they'll meet the deadline since they trust their client implicitly in the same way. So, it's possible to think that commitment to a deadline is significant to their clients. This will help you comprehend why they're upset or annoyed by their inability to finish the task in time.

Take a step back When you realize that nothing is dissuading a person's emotions Take a break from the situation and allow the situation some time. When people feel angry, their brains are flooded with chemicals, prompting them to fight or flee. It can take between 2 and 3 days for the effects of the brain chemicals to settle down. Inform the person that you have another commitment to take care of and then move on. It is also possible to inform them that you'll need some time as well as space for you to consider things through before coming back to them with an answer.

Don't let them know that you aren't prepared to solve the problem. It's about you rather than them. If you say to them that they don't have the time to discuss it immediately, they'll become more defensive. The ability to manage emotions and other people's emotions is mostly about knowing when to speak and when to remain silent in the context of the event.

Don't be reluctant to apologize If you are aware that something you've said or not, has hurt or hurt another person There's absolutely no shame in making an apology in the exact same way. Even if you were in the correct and you did end having a negative impact on the person negatively, it's appropriate to offer an apology in order to stop the situation from becoming a catastrophe.

Accept the error and apologize for it If you think it can make someone else get better at their job and ease the tension in a potentially explosive situation. It's not a sign that you are showing vulnerability, but rather a sign of emotional maturity that allows you to recognize that a more positive decision on your behalf can benefit the entire situation for all parties affected.

Take a look at the implications before taking any step , and allow yourself the chance to consider. Consider what you and your partner might feel from each possibility. Think about the consequences of every choice made by all who is involved. What will the impact be on you as well as anyone else?

What will be the impact on others affected by the incident? Are you happy with your decision? Is it in line with your values? If not, is it worthy of consideration? If you admire or admire somebody, what would this individual think of your choice? In the end, what would you prefer to see all of your peers take the same decision as you are planning to make? If not, how do you justify it?

It is essential to be aware of other people's emotions. People who are emotionally intelligent are constantly navigating by being aware of their as well as other people's feelings. Like all other skills it is possible to develop and improved.

Avoid negative personalization. Each whenever you feel negative about an event or someone else's conduct try not to jump straight to a negative conclusion and not being able to assess the situation properly. Instead, find different methods to evaluate the situation before you react. In the case of a situation, it is possible that you might be inclined to believe that someone is deliberately not paying attention to your calls if they're not responding to your messages. If we don't take everything personally, we are able to view issues in a more objective manner, which allows to make more rational decision.

Don't make everything personal. Don't make everything about you. Don't be apathetic when people do things that aren't good to you. How they behave towards you isn't reflective of them but more a reflection on them. Widen your perspective in order to lessen the possibility of misinterpretations.

Respond , don't react: Responding is an impulsive and subconscious process , where there is no control over our actions. The primary goal is to provide immediate outlet to our overwhelming emotions.

Responding involves performing in a more mindful and controlled way.

When you respond, it is important to listen to your emotions, you can decide on a your next move by analyzing not just your own but also on the other person's emotions. Once you are aware the triggers that trigger your emotions you're well-equipped to justify your actions prior to.

If, for instance, you are aware that you can get upset and start throwing temper tantrums with your coworkers and your subordinates while you're anxious about meeting an upcoming deadline, you'll be more attentive when close to a deadline in the future. You could notify your colleagues and subordinates that you're in need of time to yourself to complete your task or ease your tension. In this way, you can defuse the potential for a negative or even damaging scenario where everyone is unhappy and dissatisfied.

Keep your humility: Be humble when you interact with others who want to help you improve your control of their emotions and your expectations. If you believe that you are superior to all others and you don't make an attempt to acknowledge your shortcomings or shortcomings. You'll easily be affected by people, things and situations that don't match your expectations. You'll become angry, snappy and annoyed by things that didn't go as planned.

Take a look at things from a different viewpoint that you haven't thought of before. If you believe your spouse is a bit egocentric, think about it to imagine that they might be worried or concerned about your health. If your boss puts excessive stress on your shoulders, consider his belief that he firmly believes that you are able to be successful, which is the reason they don't want you to be below your capabilities. If your child isn't doing their best it could be because they aren't really be lazy. They might not be motivated or excited enough to learn.

Instead of continually judging other people and believing that you are superior instead, try putting yourself in the others' shoes by being gentle and thoughtful. What would you feel like when you were in the other person's shoes? What would you think, do and think about in their place? You'll be able to gain profound insights into how to handle different situations through practicing something as easy as this. Learn to be humble. You must be grounded enough to know that you're not superior to other people. Additionally, be savvy enough to know that you're unique to everyone else.

Don't be afraid of saying "no": While trying to enhance your interpersonal skills, it could have seemed as if submitting to the demands of the other party was the simplest ways to come to a agreement. While this might be true however it's not the spirit of good relationship management. It will cause your partner to be respectful of your work in the end.

Despite the negative connotations it has, refusing to be a good and essential aspect of managing relationships as it assists in restraining instinctual urges and create expectations against immediate satisfaction. It can help you reduce stress and improve how you deal with your emotions. It is also beneficial for everyone involved because you'll discover that you don't have to commit to something that you aren't able to be able to deliver. Respect you and the time that is yours. Say "no" when it's the right choice.

Be mindful of the gap Between Intention and Impact People with a lack of emotional intelligence typically fail to recognize the harmful influence their words and actions could have on others. They completely ignore the vast distance between their words and actions plan to convey and how others take their words and actions. Make sure that there is no difference between what you want to communicate and what people actually think of.

No matter what you intended to say consider the way the words you speak and your actions influence other people and if it is in tune with how you would like to affect them.

Jim was known for his rants about remarks that made people unhappy and angry. But, he slowly began taking time to reflect. He started asking himself questions like what did he want people to view his character? What impression was that he wanted to leave on others? Do he have to change the aspects of his message in order in order to get to the final outcome without becoming offended?

Engage more in the conversation How you conduct yourself in an interaction is as important as the words you use or the outcome of the conversation. Being aware of social situations means that you make an effort to show your partner that you appreciate their time as well as the conversation that you are engaging in. Take a look at your everyday interactions and consider your appearance to other people. Take a look at whether you spend the time to remove any other distractions when speaking and engaging in eye contact, and listen with an active mind rather than a passive one? Do you make the effort to seek out feedback from others on their opinions on the subject matter covered during the discussion?

Ask yourself these questions and ensure that you employ body language that is open to signal the other person you are keen to hear what they might have to say. Body language that is open includes the ability to lean forward, arms that aren't crossed, lots of eye contact, as well as smiling or laughing without having to touching the face or forming artificial barriers. Make sure your body language is in line with your words. You can also observe the other person's body language to see if they are showing signs they're not at ease in the present circumstance.

To ensure that you're communicating effectively requires taking extra time to make sure that the messages you're communicating are concise and clear and also making sure that the other person responds positively prior to moving on. Many people are reluctant to check details and facts at the conclusion of an extended conversation, in fear that it might give the impression that they're not paying to what they are saying. But the reality is that the reverse is true repeating important information at the conclusion of a discussion gives another party an impression that you are really paying attention and you want to make sure that everyone is on the same page prior to the conversation ends.

Build Trust Two Way Street: You don't expect other people to trust you if you are unable to be trusted by others. When trust is lost, it is hard to recover. Do your best in building trust with people by putting trust in them first. Be more patient and aware that humans make mistakes and are human.

When you place your trust in them, you're just encouraging others to trust you.

Encourage trust by showing a bit of trustin the first place. In this way, you'll have the ability to build stronger relationships and improve your interpersonal skills and greater emotional intelligence.

Be aware of the effect that you have on the emotions and thoughts. You must understand your impact on them in order to have an understanding of you and their feelings. Are you able to make people feel uncomfortable or angry, joyful, or anxious when you enter the room? What do they feel when you talk to them?

Examine the patterns you are observing that require change. If you are able to make lots of family members be upset or sad it is time to lower your level of anger by not throwing a punch in the face swiftly. It is possible that you need to tackle problems in a calmer, more rational way so that you can make a positive impact on the emotions of others. Receiving feedback from other people will aid you in determining the way you affect their feelings and will give you more chances to improve your emotional state.

Chapter 17: Understanding Others

When you begin to understand your feelings and how to manage them, you will be in a better position to begin examining the feelings of other people. Because you are aware that how you behave can be caused by a the lack of emotional control You will be able observe the way other people affect their emotions and how much or no emotional control takes place in a lot of settings. However, the simple realization that a lot of people behave from emotions rather than rational thought is not a guarantee that you will be able manage your behavior. This is what this chapter is all about.

• Learn how to be a good listener. Remember the hurdles you faced was the need to be a part of conversations. It is due to an instinctual wish to have your voice heard. People like to be heard to. When there is conflict, having the person have their voice heard is a great tool to ease tension. If you let your intellect to take over your observational abilities, not your emotions, you'll be amazed at how many people speak , but do not actually speak up. This will allow you to discern the important things from the white noise, and that's an essential aspect of emotional intelligence.

* Use empathy. It is important not only to listen, but you attempt to comprehend what the person you're listening to is trying to communicate. It is evident that this is usually pretty clear, but for a variety of reasons, there may be something happening that isn't being communicated. The person you're dealing with may not possess the necessary communication abilities, or there could be a motive they are hesitant to discuss explicitly. Make sure that you comprehend the spoken and non-spoken messages they're trying to convey. They might fail to convey their thoughts due to a variety of reasons. Self-importance, fear, and anger are just a few of the emotions that can impede the ability of a person to communicate. Empathy requires you to understand what

the other person is thinking and feeling. This does not mean you agree with them. Learn to understand, and then be fully understood. This will improve your standing each time.

* Listen proactively. Over ninety percent of spoken communication takes place in non-verbal. Most people do not realize the importance of our body language is, and it's especially when we are listening. We recognize that listening is essential, therefore use your body language to emphasize that you are listening. Look directly at the person you are speaking, maintain eye contactwith them, then tilt your head occasionally to indicate that you know what they're saying. Don't look down to your mobile phone, or any other mobile device when you are having an exchange. If people can see that you're willing to take the opportunity to voice their concerns and are listening, you will begin to be perceived as more approachable and friendly. The inner stress of fighting in order to make yourself heard ease and people will begin communicating efficiently and clearly. When they are more accustomed to the idea that you'll offer compassionate ear and provide them with the freedom to speak your position will go up, and so will your influence.

* Ask questions. A careful approach to questions will ensure you are fully aware of the thoughts that the other side is communicating, but it goes more than it does. It reaffirms that you've been paying attention and are interested, and that you are open to hearing a different viewpoint. It is important to resist the urge to view this as weakness for your part. If we aren't able to control our emotions, we are less inclined to listen. We fear that we will be viewed as weak, or we fear that if views that are not our own are given full expression, our standing will be diminished. Actually, the reverse is the case. When we are able to listen with empathy this strengthens our argument. We can fully comprehend the other

viewpoint, with the advantages as well as flaws. The act of asking questions can lead the attention of a skilled listener to the issues at the core of the issue. If we give the person free freedom to communicate and his thoughts, we should be able to be ourselves in the proper moment.

Be attentive to the wider audience. Often, listening is more difficult in larger groups, such as in a workplace setting. Sometimes , the person who does the majority of the talking isn't the one who best interprets the content being discussed. It is just the person who has the dominant personality. As you become more sensitive and more adept at recognizing what's happening, instead of simply focusing on who's making the most noise you'll be better in discerning between pure sound and what the actual message is. One effective way to accomplish this is to incorporate individuals who are in the margins, people who aren't very vocal and are often lost in the noise. When you invite people to participate in conversations by asking questions, a variety of elements come into the equation.

If you give voice to people who aren't always given one, you might find that some members of the group will be more open to your suggestions. In the same way you offer a platform for those who might not always agree with more affluent members but have not had the opportunity to hear their opinion heard prior to. In a subtle manner, you diminish the influence of the person who has the most powerful character by allowing a more moderate viewpoint to be heard. Instead of providing an opposing view, you might be able to convince someone else to provide the opinion of your choice for you. In the end, if you do there is nothing else to do, you be able to gain the broadest understanding possible of what feelings exist in the group.

* Don't judge others. To truly listen with empathy, we must eliminate our own judgments and feelings out of the picture. To improve your listening skills, teach

yourself to listen without judgment. Examine what's being discussed on its merits, but do not look for the correct or incorrect. This is a must in both listening to other people and also when you examine your own thought process. It may be difficult to master initially however, it's something that gets easier as you begin to distinguish the intellectual from the emotional.

Chapter 18: Empathy Intelligence and Relationships

Both intrapersonal and interpersonal skills are equally essential when it comes to relationships. For us to perform effectively when in a relationship, whether it's an intimate one, or between partners or spouses it is necessary to have excellent interpersonal and intrapersonal abilities. If you find yourself in disagreement with someone it is important to analyze your behaviour and reflect on the areas you might have gone wrong. This is a crucial step. If you're a person with strong interpersonal skills, they can aid in stopping you from getting involved in an dispute before it even starts. Additionally, you'll be more likely to finding a way to reconcile. You'll know the best way to talk to those who are in the middle of disagreement. It's true that these situations are normal. However, you might be a little unprepared to give thought to the importance of your EI is in every kind of relationship throughout your life.

Your self-reflection level is influenced by your inner capabilities. The capacity to be aware of the things you've committed wrong as well as the incorrect directions you could have taken throughout your life. The interpersonal skills, on contrary, can more clearly influence relationships and influence your interactions with the people we meet that we interact with in daily life. One method to improve your self-reflection is to record what your weaknesses and strengths are as you consider your interpersonal abilities (social awareness and management of relationships) as well as your intrapersonal abilities (self-awareness and managing yourself). You must be truthful about your own self-reflection. One of the greatest strengths we have is that are able to detect and read the moods of other people. If you're not able to read facial expressions as well as the body language of others, then you might be prone to causing offense even in ways that are not intended that could result in people's sentiments being affected. You can get better at this area by considering your facial expressions and your body language. When it comes to relationships being able to put yourself in the shoes of someone else is a crucial ability. This can help you feel empathy and comprehend the emotions that someone else may be experiencing. Are you someone who is inclined to be judgmental and self-righteous? If so, you'll need to make an effort to be more compassionate and show empathy for the person in need.

One of the fundamentals of human relationships is the ability to make people feel happy when they're within your organization. This basic idea I'm going to discuss with you will enable you think differently about your part in establishing solid human relationships. Have you ever wondered why certain individuals seem to possess the ability to attract other people, and wondered what it is that they carry within their souls? How do they work? Everybody is eager to socialize with them, chat and enjoy themselves with them, but it's not something you experience often. It is important to realize that they don't possess anything that you do not possess. The difference is in the things they can do that you cannot. You must understand that your relationship with another person begins with you. What is this? Before you start talking with someone you must already be aware of what the conversation is likely to be.

I'm talking about the emotions and feelings you feel within your body prior to starting an exciting new relationship. Be aware that each encounter with another person is the beginning of a type of relationship. Your state of mind is the most crucial aspect. If you wish for people to feel relaxed around you, or are eager to develop a relationship with you, it's essential that you give the impression of a positive attitude. If you're down and start talking to someone, they'll notice that you're negative and may not be inclined to get to know you better. People will not want to spend time with you in the event that they are feeling bad. If you radiate positive energy, others will be drawn to surround you because they feel that positive energy. They will feel the positive energy and feel happy and happy within your presence.

Before you begin to talk with others, ensure that you are in an optimistic state before opening your mouth for speaking. Your state of mind will reflect onto everyone you meet. People are likely to want to spend time with you when you give them a feeling of happiness while within your presence.

You can try this for the next few days: try to engage others with a positive outlook. They will perceive the value in it and will be inspired. You'll have the possibility of making new acquaintances who are eager to be with you.

Let's now practice some real-world exercises.

Select a negative emotion that you've felt frequently this last week. Take a seat in front of a mirror , and pretend to feel these feelings. Do what you can to actually trigger these feelings. Consider the various circumstances that triggered these negative feelings in your mind. Examine your face when you look in the mirror. What are your facial and body language reveal? Do you like the way you appear? Are you able to envision how people to perceive you? If you continue to do this exercise, you're likely to be able to recall the way you appear and this will help you to eliminate those negative feelings. Do the same exercise, but concentrate on your positive feelings. Take a look at yourself in the mirror. Do you have the appearance you want people to be able to remember you by? Do you prefer it when you appear joyful and lively instead of tense or anger? Aren't you thinking that those near you are more likely to prefer to hang out with you by displaying positive feelings and body expressions?

Take a look at your appearance when you're angry and the way you appear when you're feeling content. Make sure you create a stark distinction in your head between the two images. Consider the different emotions you might be experiencing, and the image that goes to those emotions. Try to alter your voice tone to make others think that you're in a great mood, not in a bad mood.

Chapter 19: What Things Mentally Strong People Do Not Do

Mentally strong people are the ones who are able to maintain healthy habits to strive to be better at what they do. They have the ability to take control over their emotions, thoughts and their attitudes to help them be successful both in their professional and personal lives.

For you to remain mentally robust, there are some things you have to be rid of and things you shouldn't worry about. Here are some items to stay clear of to keep and increase your mental strength

Avoid Time-Wasters

If you are determined to build your mental strength one of the initial steps you need to take is figure out the time-wasters you are, and what hinder your accomplishment. These are the issues that are keeping you from moving forward and hinder you from accomplishing the things you'd like to achieve.

Every day, people find involved in things that do not contribute to any impact on their objectives, fulfillment and overall satisfaction in life. If you are determined to achieve an emotional state then you need to determine which of your time-wasters you are and make the necessary adjustments so that you can gain the value of each minute. If you can accomplish this, you'll realize that you don't have time to spend on unnecessary things or things that are not aiding you in achieving your goals.

Everyone wants to succeed in life, however, there are some things they become entangled in that hinder their progress as they waste their time. While these issues prevent us from reaching our maximum potential, we fail to acknowledge them until someone else is able to highlight them to us.

For personal growth You must undergo the rigorous process of looking at the way you live your time. You must be able to be able to account for each second, minute and hour. Also, you should look for suggestions on how to work smarter and continuously review your daily activities to identify time-wasters. Here are some tips for making your brain stronger people do not waste time on:

Do not waste time feeling sorry for yourself

It's not doing you any good to waste the time pondering your troubles, exaggerating your shortcomings, and making reference to the struggles that you've faced.

If you're struggling to meet your financial goals or are facing some economic downturns and are looking for sympathy from others is likely only create more problems for you. It will distract you from finding the real solution to your issues and make your situation worse.

There is no way to be able to escape difficult times or suffering completely but you can definitely avoid feeling vulnerable by getting down on yourself. Even if you're unable to resolve your issues but you still have the ability to manage your reactions to the issues.

Find ways to be grateful, regardless of opponents. This will help you stay away from self-pity.

Beware of becoming addicted to Social Media

The world of social media has quickly become element of the daily life of millennials however, it's not an ideal thing to be involved in it. Everyone enjoys taking an hour or so to look up updates in Facebook, Instagram, and Twitter however, this requires an unwavering sense of control.

If you aren't in control of your time you're spending on social media sites, you'll waste lots of time observing the world of virtual reality without accomplishing everything on your list of goals.

The best way to reduce your addiction to social media or not spend time there is to establish a time restriction on your social media usage. It is possible to set the alarm or set a reminder to remind you that you have to limit your activities and then quit the app for something different. A different option would be to join to social media only after you've completed all tasks you have to complete. It could even be a reward for you completing your job.

Don't Let Your Day Go By Without a Plan

People who have a strong mental capacity are people who have plans for the tasks they have to accomplish or complete within a given day. There's a lot of value to write things down, particularly the initial two or three goals that you must accomplish within a single day. It is useless to keep a list of items because there's just too much you can accomplish in the span of all of the hours.

Be sure to break your huge tasks into manageable steps. These simple steps that form the day's plan. If you follow this method you will be able to identify a sort of desire to accomplish what you wrote down.

Avoid activities that drain your emotional energy

If you are looking to succeed in life, you must concentrate more on the factors that can have positive impacts to your lifestyle. Mentally healthy do not waste their time with things that drain their emotional energy.

Before you make the decision to take part in an activity that is on your to-do list, be sure that the project is going have a positive effect upon your daily life. If you feel that the project won't positively impact your life, think about putting it off.

Also, you should not force yourself to answer in a flash when required to perform a task. It is important to consider the consequences of doing the task before you decide to accept it. Keep in mind that it's not right to refuse certain things if you're not able to perform them.

Don't worry about things that are beyond your control

People who are mentally strong are aware that it's never a good idea to be concerned as it's not going to get them to great heights in their lives. This is particularly true for those instances where you cannot be doing anything to make any change. The best thing to do is to make sure that your thinking is centered on what you can doinstead of pondering about your inability to accomplish anything.

Avoid hanging out with negative People

It is a well-known phrase that suggests that you're like the people you make acquaintance with. The psychology of the brain says that you're the average of five people you spend the majority in your daily life with.

If you are looking to become the most perfect version of yourself make sure that you are surrounded by the most positive people you discover. Make sure you rid yourself of toxic and negative people in your life. To be successful in life it is essential to shed the burden that's always pulling you down. And negative energy emanating from those who surround you is a part of that load.

Do not give up your power

If you constantly feel as if you are the victim, you're not likely to keep your mental strength. When you are constantly thinking of thoughts that tell you that you are the victim you're giving power to other people over you.

If you are feeling like your spouse is driving you crazy or your project manager makes you feel uneasy about yourself, then what it signifies is that you are affirming that they have the ability to influence your feelings. In the ideal scenario nobody should have the power to alter your feelings, thoughts or even your actions.

The first thing to do is realize that the choice you make is entirely yours to make The only way to do this is to alter your language. Instead of saying that you have to be working late today, you could say that you've made the decision to be late for work today." While there might be consequences for not choosing to make it to work on time, you need to decide whether you want to go to work later or not.

If you've decided to stay late for work means you are still able to choose when you work and when to not.

If you are able to empower yourself to take control of your life, you'll be able to build the kind of life that you would like to live.

Don't Avoid Change

You will stick stuck in your ways and not changing if you're scared of change, because you believe it will only exacerbate your current situation. The world continues to change and your ability to succeed in life is contingent on the extent to which you're adept at adapting.

The better you are able to manage stress from various fonts, the better you will be able to build your confidence and, in the end, you're likely to gain confidence of your ability to adapt to any changes. This will enable you change your life in a positive way. You might decide to get an entirely new job or step away from relationships that are not working for you in order to learn to be flexible to change and gain other advantages.

Don't be a slave to everyone else.

If you're constantly striving to please people You will be exhausted mentally and forget about the goals you want to accomplish. It is not necessary to show off a display of who you're not to impress your parents and you don't have to go to a gathering which you normally wouldn't attend in order to not offend your mother.

It requires a lot of confidence to make decisions that may upset others particularly if they are family members However, if you are to follow your own personal rules that means you must live your life in accordance to your values and beliefs.

It is important to write your most important five values down and devote your time and energy following these values. It's true that some people don't seem to be impressed with your choices shouldn't be a reason to stop you.

Don't be afraid of taking risks

If you're afraid of something particular it is not a good idea to do it even if they're tiny. If you're on the other side you're happy with an opportunity that is new and you are not concerned about the fact that there's an element of risk and go along with the project.

Most of the time, your emotions can cloud your judgement, and this could affect your natural ability to assess the risks.

It's not possible for you to be successful in the field if you do not take risks. If you are hoping for a positive outcome, you're going to need to be willing to take risks. When you're taking risks, there's no harm in observing how you feel about the risks, and keep track of your feelings and thinking. You must make an outline of your pros and cons regarding the risk. This will allow you to make the right choice as you balance your feelings and your logic.

Don't expect quick results

Self-growth is not a quick one. If you're trying to get rid of your bad habits or improve your relationships with others or even trying to stop drinking alcohol, it is important to stay away from the lure of immediate results, as this can lead to disappointment.

Think about all the effort you put into be a marathon, not an athletic race. The bumps you're going encounter along the way as minor setbacks, not as bottlenecks.

In every stage of your life, you're going to require the mental strength is required, particularly during difficult times, such as when you lose a beloved person, or encounter setbacks in your finances, or are facing an illness. Mental strength is what that helps you be resilient and conquer the obstacles.

The great thing is that everyone has the ability to build their mental muscles, and you'll be able to continue learning how to become your own trainer to build your mental toughness. It is important to be aware of the areas where you appear to be doing very well, but take note of areas that you need to change or make improvements. Discover ways you can be more effective and set yourself the goal of becoming slightly better than you were in the last minute.

Don't make the same mistakes again.

Everyone makes mistakes. If you were embarrassed because you made a mistake in class, received a snub or ridicule for a mistake or dropped you pants on top of the entire class and it was embarrassing, the good news is that you've learned early that it's not a good idea for you to commit mistakes.

You may choose to cover up and excuse your mistakes to avoid the shame associated with these mistakes, but if make this choice, you're going to miss your opportunity for learning from mistakes.

Although you may have reverted back to the habits that you've worked so hard to eliminate or missed a crucial deadline, it is important to take every mistake as an opportunity to learn. You must let go of your pride and remain humble when evaluating the possibilities of why you did not do your best, then utilize the information you have learned from your responses to continue your journey to improve over what you used to be before.

Don't judge other people's successes

Everyone else is doing great and a friend has just purchased an automobile that you aren't able to afford and a colleague recently was promoted, or your friend has been talking about the latest accomplishments of theirs and all of this could make you feel jealous however, you should not allow jealousy to take over. If you are bewildered, you'll begin lose focus on your work and this will affect your ability to reach your objectives.

It is important to write your own vision of success, and make sure that you feel secure in your own definition of success. This will enable you stop feeling resentful towards others for having accomplished their goals and will allow you stay committed to the achievement of your goals. Always keep in mind that their successes will not diminish your chances of being successful.

Don't give up after an Initial Failing

A few people do they can to avoid failing. This is because it shows their self-worth. If you quit trying, or quit after having failed for the first time, you won't achieve your full potential.

The majority of stories about people who have achieved great success begin by describing how they tried again and did not succeed in. This should be enough incentive for you to confront your fears with confidence by pushing yourself to the limits.

In those instances when you felt devalued or even embarrassed You aren't supposed to abandon your goals. Keep your head up and never allow your mistakes or inability to achieve success to frighten or make you feel like a failure. The only thing you have to do is remain focused on improving your skills and take as many chances as you can so that you can achieve success.

Conclusion

Now you know the nature of emotions and how they influence your actions. More importantly is that you are able to manage them to build lasting and better relationships satisfaction, success, and joy in all aspects of life.

This is not the only step to being emotionally smart. Emotional perception as well as the capacity to analyze them are another crucial component of the emotional intelligence. Why? because it increases your ability to comprehend and manage your emotions with others. While focusing on your feelings is a crucial first step, being emotionally detached from the feelings of others will open up a fresh window that provides new perspectives on how to build lasting relationships.

In understanding other people and recognizing that they're similar to you and are driven by your own internal emotions, you'll be able to better understand your own. This circle will enhance your life in ways you could never have imagined before. The circular representation of your emotional intelligence which is the symbol of perfection and unity, will begin to manifest how you live your life. If you can keep your emotions and rationality in check the rest of your life will follow in the same direction.

The circle starts and is completed with your. At the end it's entirely about you. There is no one else who will be able to make these changes for you. It's your responsibility to take the necessary steps to increase your emotional intelligence. Don't quit; don't let your emotions steer you in the wrong direction. Let them guide you to happiness and success.

Be confident in your ability to manage your stress and your emotions. This is also an issue of finding the right balance. Finding the perfect mix of rationality and emotion and adhering to it, can open up a new world for you. This world will offer all the opportunities to make you happy and prosperous. It's all you need to do is get out there and take the initiative to accomplish it. You are the one who decides your destiny and create yourself luck.

www.ingramcontent.com/pod-product-compliance
Lightning Source LLC
Chambersburg PA
CBHW071836080526
44589CB00012B/1020